Media Blasting & METAL PREPARATION
A COMPLETE GUIDE

Matt Joseph

CarTech®

CarTech®

CarTech, Inc.
838 Lake Street South
Forest Lake, MN 55025
Phone: 651-277-1200 or 800-551-4754
Fax: 651-277-1203
www.cartechbooks.com

Edit by Bob Wilson
Layout by Monica Seiberlich

ISBN 978-1-61325-165-2
Item No. SA313

Library of Congress Cataloging-in-Publication Data Available

Written, edited, and designed in the U.S.A.
Printed in China
10 9 8 7 6 5 4 3 2 1

Title Page:
This is what the inside of a blast room looks like. The item under blast attack is too large to fit into a blast cabinet, which leaves an outside blasting or a blast room as the only options for blasting it. The operator is breathing outside air and is protected from blast media from head to toe.

Back Cover Photos

Top:
Soda blasting the flat back panel of this truck cab is a very safe way to remove the paint and any loose rust from it. Note the close blasting distance and very perpendicular blast angle. There isn't much rust under the paint in this area, because the paint here is pretty sound.

Upper Middle:
These red- and green-handled metering/on-off valves control the flow of each of the two types of media in Eastwood's Dual Blast system. You can make running adjustments as you blast. This is much less cumbersome than hauling two completely separate blast systems to your blast site and managing them.

Lower Middle:
For post-blasting preservation, you can apply After Blast with a plastic spray bottle. It should be allowed to sit for a short time and then wiped off. How long its protection from rust lasts depends on external factors such as temperature and humidity.

Bottom:
Removing paint and rust mechanically with a disc sander was the traditional way to strip panels. The poly disc, shown here, cuts reasonably quickly and reduces the chances of locally overheating metal. However, it cannot remove deep rust, such as the rust in the photograph, under and behind its leading edge.

DISTRIBUTION BY:

Europe
PGUK
63 Hatton Garden
London EC1N 8LE, England
Phone: 020 7061 1980 • Fax: 020 7242 3725
www.pguk.co.uk

Australia
Renniks Publications Ltd.
3/37-39 Green Street
Banksmeadow, NSW 2109, Australia
Phone: 2 9695 7055 • Fax: 2 9695 7355
www.renniks.com

CONTENTS

FOREWORD

by Chris Beebe

A renowned sports car designer, driver, and mechanic, Chris Beebe owned and operated Foreign Car Specialists in Madison, Wisconsin, from 1969 until 2014. His shop was well known for repairing unusual vehicles and employing a colorful cast of talented engineers and mechanics. His pioneering work in developing cutting-edge high-fuel-economy vehicles is less well known.

Chris and his pal Peter Egan are celebrated for their contributions to numerous *Road & Track* feature stories. His legendary racing exploits in his custom-built Lotus Super 7, Can-Am Lola T163, Lotus Elise, and other vehicles include numerous outright wins and lap records. Chris continues to work actively on an eclectic variety of interesting vehicles.

He lives in rural southern Wisconsin with his wife and two children.

As youngsters, my friends and I were interested in the automobile, not simply as a mechanism of transport. I was struck with the workings, styles, and use of them all. Before cars I had found dilapidated bicycles and scooters, those leg-pushed rigs that allowed the magic of the wheel

to come into play for a young otherwise immobile person, and I became mobile. I always enjoyed the conveyance of most anything that glided with the assistance of well-lubricated wheels, castor angled, straight axle, or non-steering, it didn't matter much, I worked with whatever it offered.

Whether the vehicle was pushed, leaned on, or propelled by an outside source, it mattered how well it worked. Along with this essential spin-off came the wish for its appearance to (at least) match its operation, and sometimes its appearance excelled. Style, color, color scheme, and condition seemed to me to have a bearing over the simplest results, and it possibly mattered to the envious eyes that fell upon it. It is likely an onlooker could see preparation exceeding that of necessity and buckle under the knowledge that he could have done more or spent more effort on his own equipment. I was the quickest kid on the block on my scruffy trike, and when it got a snappy paint job (from a discarded tin of paint) it became so good looking that no one would even race me. This sort of cosmetic antic carried on through the years of my road-racing sports cars; the preparation and presentation seemed to matter to the competition.

Matt has more than a knack for making things appear to have been correctly repaired, designed, or fabricated. He has studied, understood, and applied the necessary and detailed knowledge of the process required to all his projects. Some of the processes

he follows might seem painstakingly slow or labor-intensive to many of those wishing to repair or restore vehicles, tools, equipment, or whatever the project, but the fine results speak for themselves. He is continually reading and learning about the latest changes in product makeup, knows the dos and don'ts, how-tos, and what to watch for with filling materials, primers, prep products and the final coat of paint with its sealers. He has applied himself to knowing how to work with most common glass-fiber, steel, and aluminum panels, and will expound on others if asked.

We've known each other for decades; through the 40-some years of my owning and running Foreign Car Specialists, my repair shop in Madison, Wisconsin; through the years of his talk radio program, "All About Cars" (broadcast on WPR); and thereafter. I've leaned on Matt for his best thoughts and views because he makes a good sounding board or offers answers to whatever the question or difficulties I might face.

After exhausting all other means, I rely on Matt for a stable, well-thought-out answer to almost any question. This publication, if read, understood, and followed, will carry one through the process whatever the project, and leave a satisfying result, but for the sensitive (and personal) choice of color, that is.

This latest publication from Matt is another must-read for those interested in working on the metals of automotive bodies or chassis.

I wrote this book because over many years I have often found myself wishing that someone else had written a book like it on cleaning metal. I would have found it very helpful for much of my work on cars. Instead, I had to find out about cleaning on-the-fly by accumulating, sorting, and relating fragments of information from many different sources. I want to save you that trouble and tell you what you need to know about this topic.

Sometimes we are thrilled by thinking about our work on automobiles. Fabrication, restoration, modification, and even maintenance seem exciting. We get to solve problems, do interesting research, talk to interesting people, and, sometimes, produce things of unique beauty. It is exciting to think about these accomplishments.

Basic to all of those endeavors is cleaning metal, because automobiles accumulate grease, grime, rust, destroyed paint and plating, and many other kinds of soils. As interesting and even romantic as car projects can be, we are as likely to find ourselves facing a pile of dirty parts, scrapers, and rags with a can of solvent and a coarse-bristled brush as we are to be called on to converse with talented experts and find and apply brilliant solutions to interesting problems.

Most car projects start with dirty parts and panels and must progress through cleaning these items before much that is original and exciting can be accomplished.

The purpose of this book is two-fold: It is to help you to take advantage of the best and most appropriate cleaning techniques and processes that apply to what you are working on, and to avoid the mistakes in cleaning metal that slow down projects and that can seriously compromise results. It is likely that very few people actually enjoy the cleaning efforts inherent in car projects, but they are nonetheless there and central.

This book is intended to help you spend as little time as is necessary cleaning things and ensure that you get those things clean enough to avoid problems down the road.

The options for cleaning metal parts are numerous. In the past 75 years, new methods, including abrasive blasting, vibratory cleaning, dry ice blasting, and wet abrasive blasting have been added to traditional methods, such as disc sanding and mechanical scraping. Even-higher-tech methods of cleaning parts loom on the near horizon. This book covers both traditional and new metal cleaning methods.

Although cleaning metal may seem like a series of mundane tasks, it is much more than that. If you fail to get the metal that is the basis for your automotive projects adequately clean, you are courting mediocrity, and even disaster, in your results. Some of this is obvious, but much of it can be subtle.

Sometime after we installed a used pressure-blasting cabinet in my shop 40 years ago, I noticed that I was having difficulty with some of the soldering projects that went through our blast cabinet, such as tinning sheet metal. I didn't make the connection between the used cabinet that we had begun using and my problem getting solder to properly "wet" the metal that we cleaned in that cabinet.

I failed to make the connection between the aluminum oxide abrasive that came in our first used cabinet and my soldering problem. A salesman friend who sold abrasives happened to mention, off-handedly, to me one day that the residues from aluminum oxide abrasive could interfere with certain soldering and welding processes.

My cranial light bulb lit, and I ran some comparative experiments. Blasting with aluminum oxide media does interfere with solder and weld wetting. I wish that I had known that before I experienced the problem. It would have saved me a lot of time and frustration.

Although I cannot claim that this book will inform you about everything you need to know about cleaning metal, I promise you that between its covers is the most useful knowledge that I have gained in more than 60 years of scrubbing metal things to clean them. I hope that this will help you in your own work. After all, as someone once didn't say, "wisdom emanates from the end of a parts cleaning brush." Well, okay, someone should have said that.

Here is another example in the metal-cleaning realm of what-you-don't-know-can-hurt-you: For many years I was on a wild tear to keep silicone-containing items out of my shop. Although some silicone-based products are very good and useful, the danger of getting silicone on metal, primer, and paint is enormous. Sprayed finishes fisheye when they hit it, and that is huge issue.

Accordingly, I banned silicone waxes, conditioners, lubricants, and other formulations from our shop, in the fear that our spray booth air intake would pick up residues and

transport them onto the surfaces we were spraying. I went to great lengths to scrub bare and primed parts with silicone removing washes before topcoats were sprayed. For all of that, sometimes we still saw fisheying in our sprayed finishes.

One day, reading the specification sheet for the compressor oil that we were using, I noted that silicone was the basis of that lubricant's foam suppressant.

Wow! Against my efforts to keep silicone out of my shop and to clean it off all surfaces that we were spraying, I was sending the stuff down our air lines and depositing it on the surfaces that we blew off with compressed air to clean them. I was even using air that contained silicone to

propel paint out of our spray guns. I wish someone had told me that most compressor oils contain silicone foam suppressants. Fortunately, a few do not.

I quickly found a synthetic compressor oil that was silicone free. After a few months, and three compressor oil changes, our mysterious fisheye problems disappeared.

My hope is that this book will inform you regarding the best cleaning practices and processes, and that it will help you down the road of discovering more about all of the changing approaches to cleaning metal for yourself.

Matt Joseph
Prairie du Sac, Wisconsin

ACKNOWLEDGMENTS

Several people contributed to making this book possible with their generous contributions of time, expertise, and knowledge. They, and others too numerous to list here, made my work on this project easier and the result better. The blame for any deficiencies is mine, alone.

Charlie Ruemelin is, in many ways, the father of soda blasting in this country and around the world. Throughout his long career in abrasive blasting, and soda blasting in particular, he has contributed to the development of this technology and to expanding accurate knowledge of it. He worked hard with me, helping me to understand what soda blasting is and is not. In that process he cleared up several misconceptions that I harbored regarding soda blasting and opened my eyes to its true and great potential.

Herb Statz worked long and hard with me on much of the photography in this book and made several suggestions for improving it as we went along.

Frank Weinert, a master of abrasive blasting, generously allowed me to photograph him at his work. He also contributed greatly to my knowledge of the blasting craft.

Wayne Ayers is a master metal former and fabricator in Chetek, Wisconsin. He possesses nearly magical abilities in his field and discussed several aspects of the content of this book with me, influencing my thinking in several areas about how best to clean metal.

Rob Sinklair, who is pictured on the cover of this book, worked with me on several aspects of this book and made many useful suggestions to improve its coverage and content. He also submitted

his frame-blasting project for Chapter 7.

Chris Beebe readily consented to write the foreword and did a great job, for which I thank him.

Bob Lorkowski, proprietor of L'Cars Automotive Specialties, offered critical advice and resources when I needed them.

Herb Tobben at Clemco Industries Corporation shared his great knowledge of blasting abrasives with me. This was invaluable in expanding my knowledge of this topic.

Kurtis Ohse, also at Clemco, was a willing and useful resource for locating and providing photography of Clemco blast equipment and a great source of information on abrasive blasting in general.

Nick Capinski at the Eastwood Company helped greatly by supplying photographs of the blasting equipment, supplies, and accessories

I wish to acknowledge the contributions to this book of our ever-helpful shop cat, Ambrose. While evaluating this wood-grained dashboard for soda blasting, Ambrose decided to add his proverbial two-cents' worth. With substantial effort, I have managed to keep him out of the rest of the photos in this book.

that Eastwood sells. He did this on short notice and with great enthusiasm for my project.

Mike Doty, a highly qualified materials scientist with advanced knowledge of a wide range of coatings and, in particular, how to remove them, was kind enough to spend time with me and share his knowledge.

TuneRS Mall, the highly reputed Porsche restoration and service facility in Pompano Beach, Florida, provided a number of photos of their CryoDetail dry-ice blasting process that appear in this book.

Badger Spray & Paint Supply & Repair in Fitchburg, Wisconsin, provided me with much useful information about steam-cleaning equipment and processes, and allowed me to photograph steam-cleaning machines of many different types and capacities on their premises.

Andrew Clark of Amalgam PC in Sauk City, Wisconsin, not only kept my computer running sweetly for the duration of this writing project, but went above and beyond the call of duty solving problems with some of the graphical resources I used in this book. His advanced understanding and working knowledge of a wide variety of software and formats solved problems that baffled me. He always responded to my insoluble problems with, "We can make this work." And he always did.

Bob Wilson at CarTech was both helpful and understanding as we moved this project from concept to working idea to book. His support was continuous and valuable.

My wife of 50 years, Gail Joseph, provided all kinds of support and helped with photography when I couldn't be in two places at once (behind the camera and demonstrating a process).

Finally, my shop cat, Ambrose, tried valiantly and often to help me with photography. He only narrowly avoided being included in several of the photographs that appear in these pages. And in one case, he actually made it.

INTRODUCTION

Recently, Ford announced that starting with the 2015 model year, all F-150 regular-duty trucks would come with aluminum bodies. The F-150 is the bestselling nameplate in the United States, and this is, by far, the most ambitious venture into volume aluminum motor vehicle production in the history of the automobile. After the first dust from that announcement settled, a storm of comment ensued about repairing the large number of aluminum bodied vehicles that would soon be hitting the streets and roads.

The difficulty and cost of repairs to those bodies soon became an issue in projecting the ultimate success of Ford's F-150 aluminum alloy gamble. Major costs included training, facilities, and equipment to repair aluminum bodies. Professionals and the interested public quickly learned (if they didn't already know) the necessity of clean metal in these repairs. Aluminum and steel body work in dealership and independent shops require completely different tool sets. Of course, this applies to spot and MIG welders, but it also applies to common items, such as the hammers and dollies, that touch the surfaces of aluminum and steel body panels and structures.

You cannot cross-contaminate aluminum or steel with tools used on the other metal. If you do hit aluminum with a steel or iron hammer or dolly, or with an aluminum hammer or dolly that has previously been used on a steel panel, you have the basis for electrolytic corrosion problems buried under the finish that you build over the metal. The same sequence applies to tools used on aluminum panels, and later used on steel panels. Tools used on steel continue to be made from iron and steel, but tools used on aluminum should be made from aluminum alloys.

It gets worse.

You should not weld steel or aluminum alloy in the same area in which you weld the other metal. If you do, airborne contamination from welding and shaping one metal may contaminate the surface of the other. You need separate facilities for the two metals, or, at the very least, you need to separate welding and grinding work on the two metals with pretty sound partitions and curtains. You also need to provide separate air extraction and makeup units. It is possible that you might be able to violate these

Behold the lowly, but endlessly useful, scraper. The one in front is a World War II surplus version. It was the first tool I owned, personally. It remains on my tool cart, more than 60 years after I first used it. The scraper in back is a later, more common version of this tool.

rules in very low volume work, but as your workflow increases the risks become greater.

This example should give readers some sense of how important and how persistent the need for clean metal can be.

I entered automotive endeavors through the portal of restoration in my father's shop in the mid-1950s. As you might expect, my first jobs involved cleaning things, mostly metal things. At age 11, I didn't exactly have the knowledge, skill, dexterity, or strength to bolt down a cylinder head. Because nobody else in the shop wanted to clean parts, I was the natural and successful candidate for the job.

At first I was thrilled to be working in the shop at all. Soon, I wished that I could do the more complicated and glamorous stuff that the adults were doing, and eventually I did. However, my apprenticeship as chief cleaner and polisher lasted several years. At the time it seemed like several lifetimes.

I never disliked cleaning stamped steel parts in Stoddard solvent until my unprotected fingers tingled, sanding panels with "white gas" lubricant, or scraping and brushing the paint and rust off castings without any skin, lung, or eye protection. In fact, I kind of liked that work and always tried to perform it better and more efficiently each time it was assigned. It sure beat playing hopscotch with the other kids.

I quickly learned that different cleaning jobs required differing approaches. I learned what worked best in particular situations and how to transfer and apply that knowledge to other cleaning jobs. In return for my efforts I received what you might expect a preteenager to get in this situation, pats on my little head. I also got the great satisfaction of believing that I was beginning to know what I was doing.

From the ground floor, I came to see the cleaning racket as basic; in fact, so basic that its foundational importance was often overlooked by the older folks in the shop.

Over the years I gained considerable knowledge of and expertise in automotive cleaning work. I learned what worked well, what worked better than well, and what didn't work well, or at all. Some of this was the result of instruction, some came from my own primitive research into what worked best, and a lot of it came from good old trial and error.

Later, when I had my own shop, I continued to seek knowledge about how best to clean things in terms of efficiency and the quality of my results.

I was fascinated by abrasive blasting and experimented with all kinds of equipment configurations and blasting media. I learned which media types and sizes worked best for specific purposes and how best to apply them. I also worked with various cleaning and polishing wheels and compounds. Again, I sought efficiency and quality in applying these processes.

Tumbling and vibratory cleaning processes, among several others, interested me, and I studied them for use in both industrial and custom work settings.

Visiting other shops, I often saw cleaning jobs relegated to very low

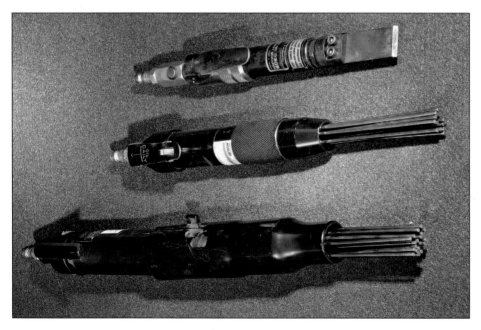

Tools such as the large and small needle scalers (bottom) and the pneumatic scraper (top) are recent versions of once-exotic industrial tools. Their prices have come down enough by now to make them practical, affordable, and very useful cleaning devices.

New kinds of surface-cleaning wheels now supplement traditional sanding disks and wire wheel and cup brushes. The flap wheel (top) and the poly wheel (bottom) remove all kinds of rust and paint quickly and almost completely. Mounted on inexpensive, small angle grinders, they are reasonably economical to use.

status, with results that were sometimes harmful to the welfare of the projects that they supported.

At some point, I realized that I had gained the necessary knowledge to write a series of articles on automotive cleaning processes. As I thought about it, I decided that a book was a better format for this material because it would present it in a single place, avoiding the fragmentation of knowledge that I had encountered in learning the cleaning crafts myself.

When I presented my idea to Bob Wilson, the editorial director at CarTech, he quickly grasped its possibilities. I think that he may have once had a brush and can of solvent in-hand, likely more than once. We both saw the potential for a book that could inform and improve practices in a very basic part of working on cars, and, by so doing, improve the quality and durability of the

work done on cars, not to mention the satisfaction of those performing the cleaning arts.

All of this had the potential to improve the efficiency and results in cleaning work. It also held the possibility of helping people who work with metal avoid some obvious but painful disasters.

In my own experience the one that comes most vividly to mind is paint failure caused by cleaning breaches or mistakes. Have you ever seen paint lifting off the area just above the roof drip rails on 1930s through 1950s restored cars? It is still pretty common. The cause is often paint remover and dip stripping chemicals that were incompletely removed from or neutralized at the seams where the drip rails attach to the roof. Another cause is failure to fully neutralize residues from the soldering fluxes used to attach those drip rails to their roofs.

These errors can be avoided if you have a good working knowledge of what clean metal is and how to achieve it.

With all of the attention paid to advanced cleaning processes, including abrasive blasting, dip stripping, and industrial vibratory cleaning, you might conclude that this book may be talking about processes and equipment that are out of your price class. Some of it probably is. But a lot of what you find here is quietly revolutionary, very useful, and available at affordable prices.

Recent arrivals to the cleaning arsenal, such as poly and flap wheels that mount on small angle grinders and small, inexpensive pneumatic scrapers and needle scalers, can make a huge difference in your cleaning practices and results.

I hope that you find the material that is presented here useful. That was my intent.

BASIC METAL
CLEANING CONSIDERATIONS

Whatever great project plans you have, if the metal on which they are based is corroded or otherwise contaminated, your plans will founder sooner rather than later. Although some factors in metal projects cannot be controlled, the surface condition of metal is largely within the range of what you can make go your way for most purposes.

I am not talking about "laboratory or metallurgically clean" here. I am describing the level of cleanliness necessary for successful painting, welding, brazing, soldering, plating, and more. If you think that there must be exceptions to the necessity for clean metal as the basis for some projects and purposes, you are probably right. Cast-iron boat anchors come readily to mind.

Is achieving clean metal easy to do? Yes and no. It depends on your facilities, your skills, your judgment, and the size and nature of what you are trying to clean. Let's survey some of the possibilities.

Underneath It All

The first consideration is the size of your object. Obviously, cleaning the metal in a piece of jewelry is very different from cleaning an auto body, which is very different from cleaning an airplane or ocean liner. In this book I stick with the jewelry-to-car size range and leave the likes of ocean liners, airplanes, and boxcars to the specialists in those fields.

The size of an item often determines what cleaning processes can and cannot be used. For example, immersion in chemical cleaners, use of electrolytic "dip tank" processes, or car factory "pickling baths" and

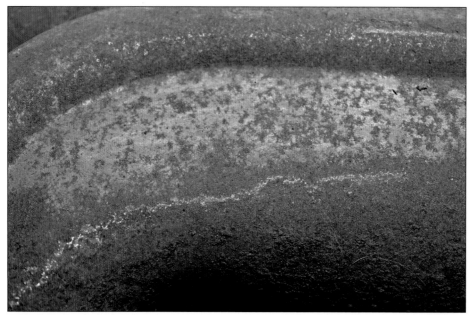

This 1930s fender provides a good example of the enemy: dirty, rusted metal. A band of metal with some paint on it is visible through the middle of the photo, with superficial rust coming through the paint. The top and bottom of the photo show flaking and deep, pitting rust.

Small parts such as this sheet-metal cover are usually much easier to clean than larger parts. Abrasive blasting, wire brushing, and chemical treatment and dipping are among the obvious ways to deal with them.

With medium-size items you may have fewer cleaning options than with very small items. After you remove grease and grime with solvent (to avoid contaminating the equipment during the next step), a trusty stationary electric wire brush wheel gives you a good start for removing rust and paint.

Large parts and panels such as this 1940s hood offer even fewer cleaning options. Dipping in chemicals is usually impractical. Even with hand-held power equipment, wire brushing tends to be too slow and less than fully effective.

Disc sanding is an obvious choice for cleaning this hood. It's reasonably fast and, if done carefully, avoids damage to the metal. This is how body panels were traditionally stripped of paint and surface rust.

Abrasive blasting with the appropriate media is another way to clean large panels, such as this hood. A lot of air and a well-isolated location are needed, too, along with considerable skill to avoid warping the sheet metal.

Small, delicate items such as this hood shutter thermostat must be handled very carefully to avoid damage. Ultrasonic cleaning works well for this part, but ultrasonic tank systems that can hold larger parts are very expensive.

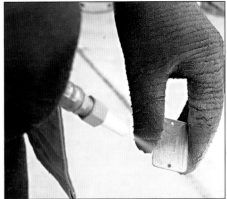

Some cleaning jobs benefit greatly from automation. The cylinder heads shown here were oven baked for 20 minutes at 400 degrees F, bombarded with steel shot (that was generated airlessly), tumbled in the device shown here to remove the shot, and then jet washed to remove any remaining contamination. The system efficiency is outstanding.

No doubt about it. This bronze emblem is very delicate. It needs special attention to get its surface down to clean metal so that its recesses can be painted and its raised sections polished. Soda blasting, shown here, is ideal to accomplish an initial, gentle cleaning.

Here's a metal-cleaning nightmare. Nothing delicate about it! This incredibly rusted cap screw should be scrapped and replaced. As rugged as it was, no amount of cleaning can return it to structural integrity. Sometimes cleaning isn't enough. It is important to know when that's the case.

Metals corrode in different ways. A badly corroded aluminum alloy step plate is shown on the left. At center is a piece of copper that is polished on its left side and in various stages of corrosion on its right side. The steel bumper cover on the right exhibits common red rust.

"e-coat" painting are practical up to the automobile end of the size range. However, ultrasonic cleaning, another liquid process, is limited to smaller parts because the cost of the equipment for this process increases radically with tank size.

Quantity is also an issue in choosing a cleaning process. I once had a contract to clean and refinish several thousand 1-inch-diameter upholstery tacks that had cast, embossed, brass heads. I determined experimentally that I could clean and refinish these items with motor-driven wire brush wheels, composition wheels, and conventional buffing equipment and compounds. This whole manual process used about five minutes of labor per tack. However, that result, 12 tacks per person/hour, was unacceptable. It would have made my bid for the job non-competitively high. Hand finishing worked fine for a dozen tacks, or even a hundred, but not for a few thousand.

Ultimately, I settled on a combination of tumbling and vibratory cleaning, followed by light hand buffing. The first two highly mechanized processes made my bid competitive. When you are cleaning batches of metal items, try to adopt a batch mentality and batch approaches.

Keep in mind that in most cases cleaning a few similar items does not demand the very high efficiency that cleaning a large number of similar items does.

The intricacy, fragility, and consistency of the object you are cleaning also make a big difference in your choice of process. Attacking an engine block with solvent and scrapers works, but so does the automated cleaning system of oven baking, shot peening, and jet washing used by many automotive machine shops. The latter, however, is simply more thorough, faster, and just plain better than poking at an engine block with solvents and scrapers. It also

has the important added advantage of relieving stress in the block's metal. Of course, there are many good approaches between those two extremes.

The kind of metal and its condition are central to your choice of the most effective cleaning approach. Ferrous metals, including steel and iron, usually take quite a beating if they are not compromised by severe corrosion or structural stress damage. They can be subjected to physically and chemically rough processes and survive intact. However, thin sections of steel, and particularly metals, including copper, aluminum, brass, and bronze, tend to be more delicate and do not take much cleaning abuse. Badly corroded steel (also known as French lace) must be cleaned very delicately to avoid damaging it beyond the possibility of repair. The same is true of badly corroded aluminum and brass, except that they often tend to be even more brittle and fragile than damaged steel.

An item such as a thin steel, brass, or bronze nameplate that is in good condition is inherently delicate and must be treated as such. Hand brushing with a soft brass or stainless-bristle wire brush, chemical cleaning, ultrasonic cleansing, or soda blasting may be the ticket to get such a piece clean enough to repair and/or refinish properly. However, blasting with a peening media, including glass bead, is likely to stretch and warp it, while attacking it with an aggressive abrasive blast media such as aluminum oxide or silicon carbide would probably be unnecessarily violent and might warp or cut through the item. Blasting with an agricultural media, such as pulverized walnut shells, peach pits, or corncobs, is slow, but mild and very useful for dealing with

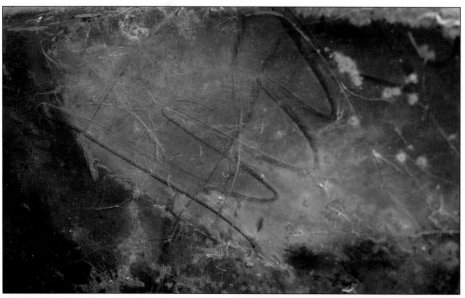

Coatings over clean metal are the first line of defense against corrosion. However, when painted surfaces are as compromised as the one shown here, the coating does no good and can accelerate the rusting process by creating protected cells under which rust propagates.

small, fragile parts. Tumbling and vibratory approaches are also possible in this case.

It is critical to keep in mind that each individual part, or batch of parts, has to be considered separately with regard to many factors (that include size, type, material, and condition) when you choose a cleaning process, or processes. Many situations benefit from the application of multiple cleaning processes. Often these processes are staged to enhance a part's safety and the cleaning result.

Types of Contamination

What you are removing from metal can be as important as the size, type, configuration, and condition of the metal itself. Contaminants

Because buffing is cleaning, buffed parts such as this nameplate may seem to be safe from contamination, except buffing wax. However, if you get fingerprints on them before you can coat and protect them, those fingerprints may develop under the coating (like the ones on an FBI wanted poster).

Welding over contamination causes defects. The top of this weld was made in cleaned metal, while its bottom was welded through dirty, rusted metal. The dirty weld has visible floating contamination in it. Furthermore, amperage variations caused by welding over contamination have bulged the surrounding metal.

This weld was allowed to age without protective coating. It shows rusting in the heat-affected zone (HAZ). That is the area from the weld out that absorbs enough heat to affect the surrounding steel. Note that the visible rusting in the HAZ is worse than that on the weld itself.

that sit on the surface of metal are easier to deal with than those that penetrate into its intricacies and pores. With the possible exception of extreme stress, corrosion is the foremost enemy of metals, and is far more common than stress damage. It is a product of metals' natural degradation, involving the tendency to combine with oxygen to form oxides. These oxides are capable of penetrating deep into and below metal surfaces and into their granular structures. In the case of steel it's called degradation "rust."

In a more general sense, corrosion is an example of the process of entropy, as described by the second law of thermodynamics. It states simply that everything in the universe tends toward a lower state of energy, sort of like a clock running down. You probably never thought of the rust that keeps trying to devour your classic Ford, Chevy, or Mopar in that sense.

Corrosion is not the exclusive disease of steel and iron. Other metals also oxidize, but without showing telltale signs of corrosion. It comes in the form of the red flakes, pits, and powders on the surfaces, the things that you associate with rust. Aluminum oxide is the product of the corrosion of aluminum and its alloys, and is white/gray in color with a powdery texture. It is every bit as deadly to aluminum alloys as rust is to ferrous metals. Copper produces a green oxidation product. Other metals show other characteristic signs of oxidation. A few metals and engineered platings do not corrode under normal conditions, but these are uncommon in the general run of automotive metal surfaces. Some of them are used to plate ferrous metals to protect them. Cadmium and cop-

per/nickel/chromium plating is commonly used for this purpose and to highlight some trim parts.

Non-magnetic stainless steel and hexavalent and trivalent plating of metallic compositions show notable resistance to corrosion. However, these are way off the beaten track of the metal surfaces that you are likely to find on automotive parts and panels.

Corrosion may be confined to just the surface of a part or panel. Superficial rust is relatively easy to remove and to prevent from recurring. Deep, pitting rust is another matter. It is difficult to eradicate it and prevent its recurrence. That's because metals have granular structures. Rust and other corrosion tend to form along the lines of grain boundaries. Once rust travels below the surface and deep into metal it becomes much more difficult to deal with, but not impossible.

Although rust is the contaminant most likely to burrow deep into metal's pores and granular structure, it is not the only contaminant that must be eradicated to achieve clean metal surfaces. Paint coatings must often, but not always, be completely removed to refinish auto body panels and parts. Grease, oil, and, silicone have to be removed from metal surfaces for painting, welding, soldering, and plating to adhere properly to them. If you try to apply paint over these impurities it fisheyes, at best. If a finish manages to cover them at all, it fails to gain proper adhesion and fails.

Silicone is particularly irksome in this regard because you cannot see it and it can be difficult to remove. Even minute amounts of silicone combat paints' surface tension and ability to cover. Solder does not wet

properly over oil, grease, and silicone, so proper tinning of surfaces becomes impossible.

Welding over contamination is in a class by itself. Okay, some welding electrodes are labeled for use on dirty and/or corroded metal. They may be capable of wetting and beading on such surfaces, but that only wins a battle, not the war. The more that you learn about hydrogen embitterment and other crack causing phenomena in weldments, the more implicated are impurities that release hydrogen and/or sulfur. Welding dirty metal is an invitation for later cracking caused by hydrogen embitterment or sulfur contamination, among several other bad possibilities.

The cleaner the metal, the better your results will be. The reasons can be complex, but the improved results that clean metal surfaces provide are often visible and dramatic.

Cleaning Methods

No one-size-fits-all prescription exists for metal cleaning processes, or how far to take them. Different jobs call for different mandates. Painting and plating are often the processes that are most intolerant of contamination. Welding is a bit more tolerant at first, but in the long run contamination can come back to bite you in the form of failed welds and cracks in the heat-affected zone (HAZ) adjacent to welds. Buffing and polishing seem to be less discriminating because they are also cleaning processes and often remove detritus that other cleaning processes have left behind.

Then, too, the standards for cleaning the metal used in your projects vary with the extent of the contamination. Here, as you might expect, rust is your toughest opponent. Although dirt, grease, paint, plating, and most other contaminants sit on the surface of metal or interlock mechanically with its surface nooks and crannies, rust is the result of a chemical reaction, and can burrow deep into metal.

In the case of some metals, such as diecast zinc, rust can form from impurities (lead, in the case of diecast zinc) in the metal. These impurities can be below the metal's surface, so the rust can originate from the inside, out. All of that makes rust and other forms of corrosion much more difficult to remove than most other contaminants. This also makes it harder to prevent their recurrence once they have started to fester.

Why and How Things Rust

Now, I need to present a small but necessary bit of rust chemistry. This will be almost painless, and definitely not a chemistry lesson. I promise.

For rust to occur, three conditions are necessary: (1) A substrate must be present. That's a surface to rust, and is a given. (2) A source of oxygen must exist as well as a medium to allow its transit to a site for rust to occur. Water, atmospheric moisture, and electrolytes, such as water contaminated with road salt, fit that bill and are ubiquitous. In the world of corrosion, you can think of electrolytes as "water on steroids." (3) A circuit must exist to move the electrons that make the conversion of metals into their corroded oxide forms possible. In the case of rust in iron and steel, this is the conversion from Fe to Fe_2O_3; that is, from iron to iron oxide, or

rust. (The chemistry is actually a bit more complicated than this and specific sequences are involved, but it roughly describes the conversion from iron to iron oxide.)

Because metals are, by their nature, electrically conductive, a circuit through them is another given.

So, the metal is a given and the circuit through it is another given, leaving only one foundation for rusting that you can manipulate: the presence of moisture or an electrolyte. The only practical way to stop rust is to deprive it of water, moisture, and, most important, electrolytes such as salty water. Okay, you have the basis for a plan. But, of course,

there are several complications in implementing it.

The first is that the substrate has to be incredibly clean before you can even consider depriving it of moisture. Here's why: If you leave any corrosion on a surface that you later coat, it contains moisture absorbed by the corrosion from the atmosphere. That moisture causes the substrate to rust further under your paint or other coating.

That's critical because rust expands to roughly 17 times the volume of the iron or steel from which it forms. Other metallic oxides have similarly disastrous displacement rates.

Why do I call them disastrous?

This panel surface was sandblasted and it then sat, unprotected, for a month. Rust specks and streaks have already appeared on it. If you try to prime and paint over them, you do so at great risk. The problem is what lies below the visible beachheads of rust.

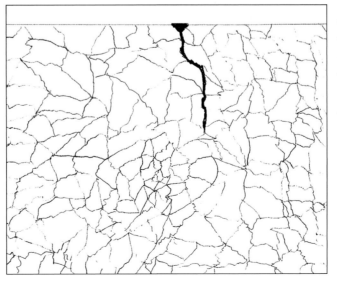

In this drawing you see a little rust spot on top of a steel surface, penetrating deep into the metal's granular structure. The penetration follows an electrical circuit along the metal's grain boundaries. This makes it very difficult to eradicate the rust completely. Small rust specks can foretell big problems.

Because metal oxides exert enormous pressures as they expand to occupy their rightful space in nature. They literally push coatings, including paint, off substrates with the greatest of ease.

To make matters even worse, coatings, such as paint, have limits of elasticity and adhesion. If you push them far enough to stretch them beyond those limits, they fracture and detach from substrates. When they fracture, the fracture lines, literally cracks in the paint, tend to act like little capillary pumps that pull water and electrolytes in under the coatings where they have detached from surfaces. This adds moisture and/or electrolytes to the rust stew that is already brewing under the coating from the original bit of corrosion that was coated over. Then, the rust festers and expands some more, using the electrical circuit(s) through the metal's granular structure that was established by the original rust that was left there under the coating.

The cracks in the finish get bigger and more cracks develop in the coat-ing. More oxygen-bearing moisture enters through them. At this point, you have a corrosion cell, a veritable rust generator, under your coating. There is no way that this little mess can do anything but get worse, and worse, and worse.

This is how and why pinhead size rust spots under paint grow to dime, quarter, and then fifty cent size sores on their way to destroying whatever they are attacking. If this sounds like the scenario for a Saturday night horror movie, it might make a great one. My choice would be Bela Lugosi or Boris Karloff to play Count Corrosion.

Do not abandon hope. In this epic battle between good and evil, well, between rust and us, remember that we are free men and women with free will, intelligence, and resolve. We can analyze the situation and fight back with proven counter-measures. We can win. We will win. Here's how.

With those two "givens," metal and a circuit through it, and one "ubiquitous," water, moisture, and/ or electrolytes, you can have only one possible plan of action, and some strategies derived from it. Your plan must be to deprive the substrate of the things that give it the oxygen that causes it to produce rust, and other oxides in other metals. Foremost among those things is water and water containing electrolytes. Your plan is to deprive substrates of these evil rust nutrients and cut the rusting process off at the pass.

Implementing this plan means removing all rust from the substrate metal so that nothing is left there to hold moisture and to promote new rust under the coatings that you place over substrates. That is the first strategy. It can never be accomplished perfectly, but the cleaner you get your base metal, the less likely it is to rust after it is coated.

The second strategy is to either convert the clean substrate to something other than rust that is so chemically stable that oxygen is unlikely to displace it and then combine with the substrate metal to

Ospho is one of many available metal preps and conditioners. I've always had good results using it to protect unpainted steel surfaces until I can apply a finish to them. Ospho improves paint adhesion, too, by etching metal surfaces. Always rinse Ospho off with water before it dries.

Every major paint company offers one or more reactive (etching or self-etching) primers. DuPont's Vari-Prime is a two-part epoxy self-etching primer that provides a terrific foundation for finishes when applied over clean metal. Never use any reactive primer over a rust converter, conditioner, or prep such as Ospho.

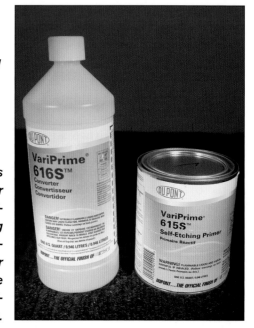

create new rust or other *undesirable* oxides. "How do I do that?" you ask. You can do that by converting it to *more desirable* oxides.

The third and final strategy is to coat either the clean or converted substrate with a coating that moisture and electrolytes cannot easily penetrate.

Most of this book concerns the first strategy, making metal so clean that there is not enough remaining corrosion to start a corrosion cell. That is always the first-line defense in preventing corrosion from attacking your work.

The second strategy, converting the surface of the substrate to

Aerosol self-etching primers are widely available and much less expensive than the automotive paint company products in this range. Although they are less effective and durable than those products, they still manage to do a very credible job, and with much less application fuss and expense.

something that rust does not attack, has several branches. In the past, so-called "conversion coatings" and "rust converters" employing phosphoric acid, tannic acid, and other agents have been the most usual way to accomplish this strategy. These coatings work very much like the gun bluing that converts iron and steel surfaces to Fe_3O_4, a stable blue/black finish that protects against rusting. There are many conversion coatings on the market. Automotive paint manufacturers offer some of them as parts of anti-corrosion finishing systems. These are often called "metal conditioners" and "metal preps."

Another class of products that converts steel surfaces to more stable oxide forms is reactive primers. These are usually epoxy based and are available in one- and two-part formats. They are designed to coat and react with substrates to form mechanical and chemical bonds with them. This produces a conversion of the surface under the coatings to an oxide of steel/iron that is not the common rust degradation oxide for the metal. Reactive primers also tend to be very molecularly dense and, therefore, resistant to the transit of water molecules through them. (Conventional sanding primers do not have that kind of density and

offer virtually no protection for base metal until they are top coated with denser finish coats.) Reactive primers provide another way to deprive substrate metals of the oxygen that they require for corrosion, while changing the metal in the surface to a format that strongly resists corrosion.

It should be noted that conversion coatings, metal preps, and metal conditioners should never be used under reactive primers. Each member of this class of anti-corrosion treatments and coatings is a sole measure that cannot be combined with other chemically reactive metal conditioning and coating measures.

The third strategy is to cover the cleaned and/or converted metal surfaces with coatings that are so impervious to the transit of water molecules that even without converting their surfaces to a more stable form than the base metal, the coating protects them from corrosive molecules. Moisture-cure urethanes are notable for success in this mission. They are also very tough and resilient to abrasion. However, they may lack strong resistance to ultraviolet light, and they do not possess the physical qualities to make them good topcoat finishes. Their resilient toughness results from their softness, making them difficult or impossible to sand as primer coats.

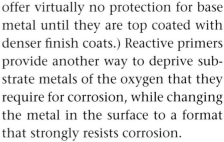

Slow-dry enamel primers and paints, such as the legendary Corroless, encapsulate and isolate rust. The deservedly highly reputed Rust-Oleum products also do a good job penetrating and encapsulating minor rust, and preventing its propagation. Fortified slow-dry enamels such as these have many good uses but are not suitable as automotive topcoats.

A variant of the impervious-to-moisture coating strategy involves using products that isolate and stop rust without converting it, and then encapsulate the rust to prevent moisture from getting to it and causing further rusting. The best known in this subset of barrier coating products are oil-based slow drying enamels. Some of these have origin in exotic settings, including coating the insides of pipelines. Others are fairly common and can be found on the shelves of your local hardware, building, or farm store. These products are fortified with various additives to help them penetrate light rust and neutralize it. Some of them work very well, but none produces an automotive-quality finish. However, if you are painting something like a water pump, bellhousing, or flywheel cover, these products work quite well and can tolerate small amounts of rust under them for surprisingly long periods. They are the coatings of choice if you cannot resist the temptation to paint over a speck, or speckles, of rust.

Clearly, the first and most important step in preventing corrosion is to start with the cleanest possible surface, before any coating is applied over it. That is the basic defense and gold standard of fighting rust. Conversion coatings and reactive primers offer further insurance against corrosion. They should be seen as very useful secondary strategies in the war against rust. Fortified slow drying oil-based enamel is another tool for fighting rust in some situations.

The Battle Against Rust

We know that clean metal is critical to success with metal projects.

But the question remains, how clean does metal have to be? The simple answer is, as clean as it is practical to get it. That means that you should do everything you can reasonably do to remove contaminants from metal surfaces and to prevent them from being re-deposited on those surfaces before you convert and/or coat them. That sounds pretty flat-footed simple, and it is. Regardless of how good your secondary lines of defense against corrosion are, your primary defense is always clean metal. The temptation to leave a speck of dirt or rust on a surface, and hope that your conversion coating, reactive primer, or slow dry enamel takes care of it is, most often, a temporary fix and an illusion. However, truly clean metal is virtually unattainable in some places and situations.

Take, for example, the crimped door skin or decklid seams at the edges of those panels. From a corrosion/clean metal point of view they are disasters waiting to happen.

In many climates, these seam areas are subjected to the winter assault of one of the world's truly great corrosion electrolytes, salty water. It is propelled toward them at high velocity in aerosolized form by the tires of oncoming and passing vehicles. Moisture condenses inside these crimped edge panels and combines with the dirt and debris that has become resident there. This crud-laden brew runs down the panel's insides to their bottoms, where it sits on the inside tops of the bottom crimped seams.

Typically, dirt and debris have already collected there. And there they act like sponges to hold liquid contaminants against the inside of the crimped seams. What gravity and vibration don't do to draw this awful

mishmash further into the seam, capillary action accomplishes. And, of course, the assault by salty water is simultaneously taking place on the outsides of these crimped seams.

Now, there's a whole galaxy of new things to worry about as you drive through the snow and slush.

Without taking such seams apart, no practical way exists to determine if the metal in them has been adequately cleaned. Worse, you have no way to determine that corrosion hasn't started to attack them, unless, of course, the area is already so badly and visibly damaged that it is necessary to apply a new panel skin, or to section in new metal to replace the old seam metal. Any method of cleaning that goes deep enough into the seam to eradicate most of the potential rust there, such as a chemical immersion approach, tends to leave residues that are extremely difficult to remove or neutralize. That kind of contamination can lift any coating that you try to apply over such crimped seam areas.

In this case, the best solution is to get the area as externally clean as you can, and then to seal it as completely as possible against the further entry by water and electrolytes. Moisture-cure urethanes that come in liquid and paste formats (paints, "seam sealers," and caulks) are good for this because they are relatively impervious to transit by water and other liquids, and they tend to leach moisture from substrates as they initiate their cures. Anti-corrosion sealing products, such as foams and gels (that are not based on moisture-cure sequences) claim to displace water and moisture, and to seal against their re-entry. Hot-applied undercoating products based on paraffin waxes and fortified with corrosion

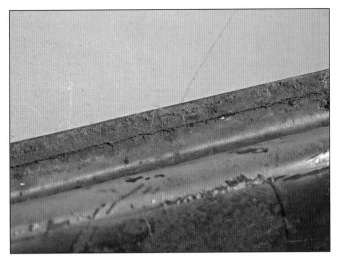

The only sure way to stop the rust in this decklid seam is to remove the skin and replace it, or to repair its damaged areas with new metal. Cleaning the area thoroughly and applying moisture-cure urethane paint or seam sealer to the exposed outside joint may work temporarily.

inhibitors can also be very effective in these situations.

Happily, areas such as panel edge seams are exceptional in the difficulties they present in cleaning and sealing. Most surfaces on cars are easier to inspect and clean. Take, for example, the outer surface of an auto body panel, including a fender or a hood. The metal in them is almost completely accessible, either mounted on a car or removed from it.

How clean does a fender or hood have to be before you can weld or paint it? Here's a hint before you try to answer that one. ("Perfectly" isn't the right answer, because that is an unattainable state in the real world of cleaning.) In fact, that fender or hood surface doesn't have to be "laboratory" or "metallurgically" clean to weld it or to have it hold paint

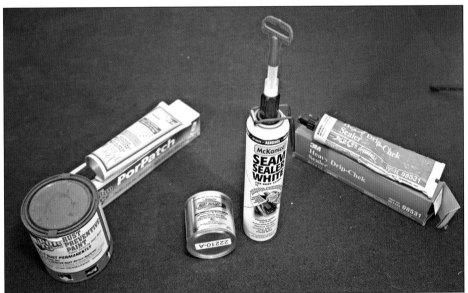

Seam-sealing products such as these are designed to seal crimped seams. The two on the left from POR 15 are intended for application over rusty metal. They leach moisture out of rusty seams and protect them with a dense, waterproof coating.

Solvent parts baths such as this one are mainstays for cleaning mechanical parts. They perform well in that role if sediment is removed from them regularly and their solvents are replaced when they become contaminated. They should never be the final step in cleaning for painting.

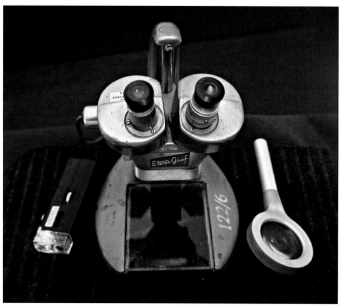

The 3D microscope in the center lets you look at metal surfaces far beyond what you need to inspect for decontamination. However, the small, handheld, illuminated pocket microscope (left) and the illuminated magnifying glass (right) are great tools for inspecting metal surfaces for cleanliness.

Metal wiping solutions such as DuPont Prep-Sol do an excellent job of removing oil, grease, and particularly, silicone from metal surfaces. Less expensive fluids including trichlorethane-based brake cleaners and enamel reducers also remove oil and grease but do not remove silicone residues as completely as do wiping solutions from paint companies.

reliably. But it will likely need to be as clean as you can get it for those purposes.

How clean something looks and how clean it is are usually critically different. Paint and rust are at the easy end of the scale of contaminants that you have to remove from metal. You can pretty much see where they are and when they have been mostly removed. Or can you? If you carry your inspection to a microscopic level you often see remnants of things that you thought you had thoroughly expunged.

Then there are contaminants like oil, grease, and silicon. They tend to be invisible to the unaided eye. Yet any of them in small concentration can cause paint to fisheye and/or to lack adhesion. Even the fingerprint of anyone guilty of touching unprotected metal deposits enough body oils and moisture to become a potential cause of painting defects.

Some contamination does not attack surfaces from the outside; it lurks beneath them. For example, lead impurity in some diecast zinc items, such as trim and door han-

dles, can corrode these parts from the inside out. In this case, corrosion cells start beneath the surface and work out. Removing all traces of corrosive contaminants from these parts' surfaces and subsurfaces is challenging in the extreme.

The truth is that while you can never get anything absolutely clean, it doesn't hurt to try, even if you never achieve it. At best you will dilute contamination from the surfaces of metal to levels that are not a problem for your next steps: welding, painting, plating, etc. This doesn't sound very elegant or hopeful, but it is very serviceable. Get metal surfaces as clean as you can, but realize that there is always something left lurking on them. If you dilute that something sufficiently, you have used a tactic that will probably win your war.

In the case of rust, you may leave some of it behind, but if you convert the metal surface to a stable form that is not rust, you have again used a tactic that gives you an excellent chance of winning your battle with corrosion.

Use a metal wash to remove oils and silicone before you apply a metal converter solution or etching primer; it will likely save your project from defeat by some insidious and largely invisible enemy of paint adhesion.

Barrier coatings such as moisture-cure urethane paint paste or caulk leach moisture out of a substrate and are great weapons in your battle.

Employing a slow-dry enamel to encapsulate and isolate rust is also a serviceable strategy against corrosion.

None of these weapons or tactics results in outright, automatic, or irreversible wins, but if they allow you to take enough of the rust enemy prisoner, you will likely win the war with corrosion for a very long time.

BASIC APPROACHES TO CLEANING METAL

"Scratch, scratch." That's the sound of cleaning metal. Okay, you can't always hear it, and it doesn't always sound just like that, but abrasion is the key; it is, literally, the only way that you can clean metal.

"Sure," you say, "that covers the old routines: wire brush, sanding disk, abrasive blasting, and the like, but what about laser, ultra-sonic, and chemical cleaning, and other approaches that don't seem to scratch anything?"

In truth, all cleaning methods involve abrasion at some level, mighty or small. Once you get beyond the obvious abrasive methods, the abrasion tends to be subtler, but it's still abrasion. Approaches such as sanding, abrasive blasting, buffing, and polishing may keep the scratching at sub-visible levels, but they don't eliminate it.

I'm not saying that the mean old iceberg was just trying to clean the poor Titanic's hull, but you *could* look at it that way.

Take these examples: solvent and ultrasonic cleaning. In the first case, the scrubbing is done by the natural action of solvent molecules against surfaces and the things that contaminate them.

In the case of ultrasonic cleansing, the machines that do it tend to emit a slight, audible hum and hiss, but that isn't the part of the sound spectrum that is actually doing the cleaning. In an ultrasonic cleaning tank, shock waves that are invisible to the eye and soundless to the ear

Behold the most basic of automotive cleaning processes: good old solvent and a bristle brush. What it lacks in high tech shock, awe, and pizzazz, it makes up by being inexpensive, effective, and dependable. The solvent loosens and dissolves dirt and grime and the bristle brush pushes it off surfaces.

This thoroughly modern ultrasonic cleaning tank is used for cleaning aluminum engine parts at Weaver Automotive Supply in Sauk City, Wisconsin. Transducers generate ultrasonic waves in a heated chemical solution to scrub parts clean. Run cycles are timed. Cleaning is usually completed in less than an hour.

Pumped solvent allows you to stream cleaning solvents over parts to remove contamination. In this case a stiff bristled brush is being used to add cleaning umph to the process. This approach isn't high tech, but it is effective.

are imploding water-based cleaning agents against the tank and its contents, and cavitating those surfaces that are in contact with them and the liquid cleaning agent.

This exposes the tank and its contents to the very raw ends of very bipolar water molecules. Those molecules scratch away at surfaces at a molecular level and cleanse them of any loose materials that are adhering to them.

The same process, cavitation, sometimes afflicts the high-speed end surfaces of marine propellers. Those areas simply move through the water faster than it can fill the cavities that their rapid motion opens. You may have seen the result of this process: propeller trailing-end surfaces that look like the Loch Ness Monster had been chewing on them. In fact, this is damage at a molecular level, caused by imploding water. Of course, in an ultrasonic cleaning tank the action is tuned and calibrated to be much milder and less destructive than that.

Ultrasonic cleaning is extremely effective for small parts and parts up to the range of cylinder heads and

Overspinning this bronze propeller caused water to cavitate its trailing edge. The same ultrasonic process is used to clean metal in ultrasonic cleaning tanks. Of course, in those tanks its intensity is controlled and held below levels that would damage metal.

This small ultrasonic cleaner features a timer and some serious ultrasonic cleaning power. It is ideal for cleaning items such as this delicate brass ether-filled hood shutter bellows. Warm water and detergent make the bellows almost shiny clean without endangering its integrity.

This radiator hot tank is typical of heated solvent tanks used to clean large parts. The solvent used here is water based and removes many kinds of grime from surfaces. It is terrific for getting into and cleaning complex items, such as radiators.

radiators. It sounds very high tech, and it is. But the basis for it is still scratch, scratch, abrasion. Always keep in mind that some form of abrasion is the basis of all metal cleaning procedures and processes.

Chemical Liquid Parts Baths

Liquid solvent cleaning is basic to all car shops. The old "parts bath" has been around for as long as parts and machinery have needed cleaning. The most basic solvents have been based on petroleum. Stoddard solvent, an aliphatic and alicyclic hydrocarbon concoction, has been around in various formulations since at least the 1920s, when it began to replace turpentine as the preferred mechanical shop cleaning solvent.

Carbon tetrachloride was also used widely in automotive shops, especially to cleanse brake and clutch friction surfaces, and in other areas where oily residues cannot be tolerated. In recent decades "carbon tet," as it was commonly known, has been unavailable for this purpose because of evidence that it is carcinogenic, and particularly, implicated in causing liver cancer.

The market carries two replacements for carbon tet. The most common is a closely related chlorinated solvent, tetrachloroethylene, which looks, smells, and acts very much like carbon tet. This solvent is sold under many brand names as "brake cleaner."

The new kid on the block in degreasing solvents is "green brake cleaner." Again, this type of product is sold under many brand names and typically is made up of the same components often found in enamel reducers and lacquer thinners, acetone and toluene, plus a few other solvents, such as methanol, but in very different proportions from those in reducers and thinners.

In the past three or four decades, water-based parts cleaning and degreasing solutions have become common in shops. They are beginning to replace petroleum-based solvents as the mainstays of parts cleaning. Some of these products require heating for maximum effectiveness, and many of them are most effective when they are hosed over parts. Formulas for water-based cleaning solvents vary. Some are based on citric acid; others rely primarily on aggressive detergents.

Another class of cleaning and metal conditioning agents known as layered cleaning solutions, or hydroseal treatments, was once widely available for cleaning carburetors, fuel pumps, and other fuel system parts. Marketed under such names as Bendix Speedclean, Bendix Metalclean, Thyme, and Gunk, these solutions had several layers to clean and seal the porosities in metal, particularly the diecast zinc used to make major carburetor, fuel pump, and other fuel system components. Most modern versions of these cleaners lack the elaborate layering of solutions that made the older

Super Agitene is a petroleum-based general-purpose parts wash that is milder than Stoddard Solvent. It is intended for pumped-stream parts wash units and even contains lanolin to reduce skin irritation from solvent drying, although you should always wear protective gloves when using any liquid solvent.

The Stoddard Solvent in this barrel was once the standard approach to cleaning metal parts. Petroleum based, it was very effective at removing many kinds of oily grime, but not paint and rust. Because it is harmful to humans and the environment, water-based solvents have largely replaced it.

Brakleen comes in traditional and "green" varieties. The traditional concoction has some similarities to carbon tetrachloride (now banned). It contains tetrachloroethylene and is a terrific fast-drying degreaser. CRC Green Brakleen is based on non-chlorinated solvents, similar to those in lacquer thinner. It is also a good degreaser.

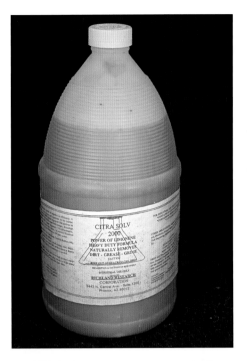

Citra Solv 2000 (now just called Citra Solv) was one of the earliest industrial citrus-based solvents. Made from volatile chemicals in orange rinds, it can be diluted with water in many ratios and is great for removing grease and grime quickly and thoroughly. However, it can harm some plastics and rubbers.

Oil Eater sprayable solvents are two of the many non-petroleum-based products. They do very well removing surface grease and are safe for most materials, including human skin. As with any effective solvent, it is important to keep them out of your eyes and to avoid prolonged skin contact.

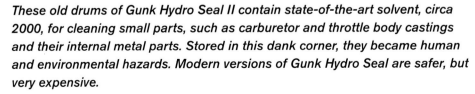

These old drums of Gunk Hydro Seal II contain state-of-the-art solvent, circa 2000, for cleaning small parts, such as carburetor and throttle body castings and their internal metal parts. Stored in this dank corner, they became human and environmental hazards. Modern versions of Gunk Hydro Seal are safer, but very expensive.

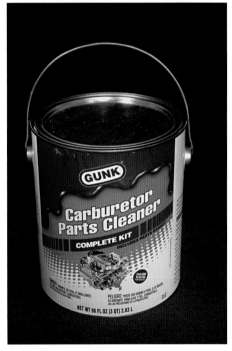

Modern Gunk Carburetor Parts Cleaner is a good and relatively inexpensive immersion cleaner that is milder than the Hydro Seal II–type layered carburetor cleaners. It lacks the ability to seal porosities in die-cast metal parts, one of the features of some of the older carburetor cleaners.

formulations both effective and environmentally problematic.

To use these layered cleaners, parts were placed in metal mesh baskets and lowered into the bottoms of the drums (usually 5-gallon capacity) in which these cleaners were shipped. In a matter of hours, soils such as carbon, varnish, paint, and more were dissolved and removed. The time required depended on which product you used and how dirty the parts were. It also depended on the temperature of the solution.

After an hour to a day, the parts were pulled up through the solutions. Each layer of the solution had a different function. Cleaning layers dissolved and removed soil. Coating layers sealed porosities in the metal surfaces. The top layer was always water. Water was always the final rinse cleaner; it kept the volatiles in the chemicals below from evaporating.

These were marvelously effective cleaners, but they contained several dangerous components that caused environmental degradation. Most of them went out of manufacture decades ago. One exception is Gunk Hydro Seal II, which, while it is a terrific solvent, lacks some of the intricate and sophisticated chemistry of the earlier solvents of this type. It is also quite expensive.

I go into detail on the old layered fuel system parts cleaners because you may find references to using them in old rebuild manuals. For all practical purposes, these products no longer exist in anything like their original formulations, and it is best to find other, more modern approaches to cleaning the kinds of parts for which they were designed and/or specified. Actually, the external diecast fuel pumps and complex carburetors for which these cleaners were developed have also been absent from automotive production since the demise, decades ago, of non-submersible fuel pumps and throttle body injection systems.

Electrolytic and Chemical Processes

Electrolytic cleaning is generally considered an industrial process. It has applications in fields such as electroplating where current is run between anodes and cathodes attached to parts suspended in chemical solutions. Names for this process in plating vary. "Pickling" and "reverse plating" are among the most common monikers for it.

In electrolytic cleaning processes, parts are attached to the anode (-, in the case of reverse plating) in the system. Current flows to the cathode (+, in the case of reverse plating), which is in circuit with a conductive acid bath in which the parts are immersed. The result is to remove molecules of conductive contaminants, such as old plating, from the parts and deposit them on the metal cathode in the plating solution. For the most part, and with very few exceptions, "Don't try this at home."

Reverse plating can be accomplished safely with low voltages and weak acids for cleaning very small parts in preparation for brush plating them. Think in the range of small screws or washers. However, to try to clean a large part, such as a water pump casting, would be both dangerous and ineffective in a non-commercial setting. These processes are well beyond the common cleaning needs of most automotive shop work and are the province of specialized operators with very expensive equipment that requires very strong safety measures. Relatively high current flows and harsh chemicals are also characteristic of cleaning processes for plating.

The same cautions apply to immersion, or "dip" stripping. Once popular with car restorers, commercial dip stripping tanks have become a rarity in the last two or three decades. In this process, heated chemical baths that are much less acidic and aggressive than those used in reverse plating were used to strip large parts, such as fenders and even whole frames and raw unitized bodies, of rust, paint, and other contaminants. These items were totally immersed in a cleaning solution and a current was run through them to dissolve and unbond their contaminants into the fluid. The same anode/cathode setup was used as in reverse plating, but the chemical baths were very different in composition.

This once common process ran into multiple problems and survives mostly as an industrial cleaning method today.

One problem involved the lead-based paints that were stripped from old auto bodies and parts this way. It was very difficult to responsibly and legally dispose of the contaminated immersion fluids containing lead primer and paint residues.

Another problem involved completely removing the cleaning agents from the cleaned parts. They had a tendency to remain in auto body seams and other nooks and crannies, and to lift the finishes applied over them.

Sometimes, six months to a year after dip stripping and refinishing, paint was lifting in problem areas, such as roof drip rail seams and rear quarter panel seams.

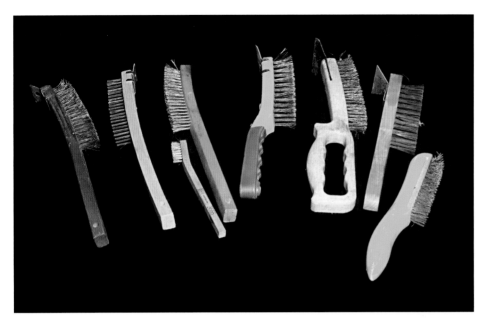

Low tech but very useful. Left to right: two wood-handled high-carbon steel bristled wire brushes, small and large stainless steel bristled brushes, two plastic-handled stainless steel bristled brushes, a large wood-handled carbon steel bristled brush, and a plastic-handled brass bristled brush.

The hand wire brush is still one of the best approaches to the first mechanical cleaning of very dirty, rusty small parts. It removes the loose stuff quickly and efficiently, without damaging most surfaces. Other cleaning processes usually follow the hand wire brush and solvent routine.

The best dip stripping providers solved some of these problems and managed to do better at neutralizing the stripping chemicals on their finished work. Today, they are able to solve many of the issues that dogged them in the past. Dip stripping continues on a much-reduced scale from its heyday in the 1970s and 1980s. Unfortunately, the reduced number of suppliers of this service and their increased costs in conforming to environmental mandates has made dip stripping an expensive way to cleanse auto bodies.

Mechanical Abrasives

The list of mechanical, non–media-blasting methods for abrading the surfaces of metal for cleaning purposes is extensive, to say the least. The field of human mechanical-abrasive metal cleaning was born when someone first rubbed sand or pebbles over some object to clean or brighten it, such as to remove the scale from a piece of hammer-forged copper in the Copper Age (5,000 to 3,500 BC). Through the years, its advance has involved some of the human mind's most imaginative, inventive, and ingenious efforts.

The basic proposition here is to drag, motor, or vibrate something with a sharp surface texture or with many sharp edges over a surface to remove contamination from the second surface and/or to impart specific surface characteristics to it. Abraded surfaces can be designed to achieve specific objectives such as holding paint or ease of later polishing.

The size, material, shape, and method of movement of the abrading media are among the many variables in this proposition. Anything from a simple scraper to a piece of

This flex-shaft–driven rotary wire brush is faster than any hand wire brush. It quickly removes loose rust and grime from metal surfaces but is a bit awkward for working into intricate areas. It does wonders cleaning large, accessible surfaces. This cleaning method requires later sanding for good paint adhesion.

The combinations of air and electric angle grinders of many sizes, fitted with rotary brushes of many configurations and materials, are many. Left-to-right: electric-driven twisted wire brush, air-driven fine wire cup brush, large electric-driven coarse wire cup brush, and electric-driven fine brass cup brush.

sandpaper fits the bill, but so, too, does advanced vibratory cleaning and many ingenious types of mechanically driven abrasive papers, wheels, and discs. The possibilities for mechanically delivering abrasives of many types to surfaces are endless.

Most basic among mechanical abrasive processes are those that are designed to remove loose contaminants from surfaces, often in preparation for more extensive and thorough cleaning processes. These sometimes follow, or are used in concert with, initial non-mechanical abrasive processes, including fluid degreasing, chemical coating removal, pressure washing, steam cleaning, and the like.

Hand wire brushing is very basic among these processes, and the brushes are available bristled with various materials such as stainless steel or high-carbon steel. Over the years, I have discovered that stainless bristled ends tend to round and dull much more quickly than carbon steel bristles, and while stainless steel "anything" has great advertising appeal and cachet, carbon steel–bristled cleaning brushes tend to be superior for cleaning auto parts because they hold their edges better than stainless bristled brushes do. They are often cheaper, too. Brass bristled wire brushes are more effective than nylon bristled brushes and nowhere near as harsh as steel bristled brushes. Keep this in mind when you are dealing with delicate or easily scratched surfaces.

Hand wire brushing is a slow, wholly manual process that is great for working very carefully on awkward shapes, or through limited accesses. Power wire brushing is much faster and can clear large areas of surface fairly quickly and efficiently.

However, it tends to polish surfaces and does not produce good conditions for adhering paint. Often, light sanding after power wire brushing corrects this problem. Bristle types for power brushing include steel, brass, plastic (the latter sometimes containing inclusions of hard granular particles to enhance cleaning power), and other materials. These brushes can be arranged in various configurations, such as cup brushes, flat brushes, braided brushes, etc. Wheel diameter can vary, as can bristle configuration, diameter, and stiffness. Twisted bristle brushes are often used for heavy-duty applications. Bristled brushes can be driven at varying speeds, applied with varying pressures, and driven by many different devices, such as handheld grinders, drill motors, flex shaft devices, etc.

In general, the best selections amongst these possibilities are derived from common sense and experience. For example, brass bristles are best for use on delicate metal surfaces because they tend to be soft and non-marring. Likewise, low application pressure and low motor speed (approximately 1,750 rpm or less versus 3,400 rpm or more) is generally best for these surfaces. On the other hand, braided steel brushes with large-diameter, stiff bristles work best for removing a lot of strongly adhered surface contamination from items such as rough castings and badly corroded thick steel sections.

I know of no simple guide to selecting the best rotary brush or drive system for a job other than what I mentioned: experience and common sense.

Abrasive coated paper ("sandpaper") is another mainstay of abrasive cleaning. This can be as simple as using a board, pad, block, or paddle to back up abrasive paper, or as fancy as employing various mechanical devices to back up and move the paper.

In traditional hand sanding the paper or other abrasive-laden media

Rotary brushes come in many sizes, configurations, and bristle types. Shown here: large twisted fine wire and coarse flat wire brushes. Small flat wire, brass bristled, and twisted wire flat brushes, as well as, of course, flat wire and twisted wire cup brushes. See if you can identify each of them.

Metal can be mechanically cleaned in many different ways. Some methods are better than others. This power wire brush is very good for some purposes, but not for this one. It's a slow and inefficient way to remove paint and rust from this brake drum. Abrasive blasting is a better choice.

is backed up with something of varying hardness, depending on how much detail you want to preserve in the surface you are sanding.

Softer backings, such as foam rubber, tend to retain detail in sanded surfaces better, while harder backings, such as hard rubber and wood, tend to flatten surfaces better. Using bare fingers to back up abrasive papers is a bad approach because the pressure points on your fingertips sand small ridges into the surface. Always back up abrasive paper with an appropriate backing material for what you are sanding. In most cases it is best to hold abrasive paper in, or around, some kind of holder.

Basic hand sanding tools. Bottom, left to right: a foam backing pad, a hard rubber pad, and a shaped abrasive sponge. Center, far left: two shaped sandpaper holders, a rubber sanding block, and a long board sander. Top, left to right: a short board sander and a flexible board sander.

Power sanders come in many types. Shown here: (far left) an air inline sander. To its right, top to bottom: an air rotary sander, an air dual-action (DA) sander, and another air disc sander. Far right, top to bottom: a narrow air belt sander, an air jitterbug sander, and an electric orbital sander.

This 3-inch-diameter rubber drum sander is useful for a variety of metal cleaning jobs when you want to go deep. It has a somewhat pliable backing that, with light pressure, removes surface pitting and rust without damaging parts. Woodworking supply stores sell 3-inch sanding sleeves for it.

This large, 6-inch-diameter Ekstrom-Carlson pneumatic drum sander is ideal for slowly removing hard coatings. Its air-filled bladder conforms to mild contours, such as the major shapes in this manifold, and cleans and surfaces them effectively. It is shown here removing porcelain residues.

Sanding boards are designed to remove material and to flatten and true wavy surfaces. If you use them correctly, they work very well. Flexible sanding boards are very good for following broad curves that are not compound curves. Various forms of sanding blocks can be used to advantage for both of these purposes.

Powered sanding devices come in many types and configurations. Disc, dual action (DA), and jitterbug are the most useful for automotive metal cleaning work. Others, such as stationary pneumatic drum sanders and wheels with brush-backed abrasive paper strips, are highly specialized but very useful for sanding automotive parts in particular situations. Items such as sandpaper flails look great but have very little useful application to any kind of real-world sanding. At least, I have yet to find many valid uses for them.

Master the art of sanding with disc, DA, and jitterbug sanding devices, and you will have mastered the most useful sanding devices that exist for working with automotive metal. Disc sanding, in particular, demands serious learning to perform effectively. You can do a lot of good or damage with a disc sander. The

The disc/belt sander in front is handy for surface removal and serious leveling when you want to remove a lot of surface. The sanding belt also levels surfaces well. Discs have more velocity at their outer edges, making them difficult to use consistently. Note the spindle sander in the background.

This disc/belt sander uses an unbacked belt that can be made of any grade and grit of sandpaper, or even of Scotch-Brite or cotton polishing belting. The belt is spring tensioned and conforms readily to curved surfaces. This makes it a quick and safe tool for removing surface contamination.

This 12-inch Vonnegut-Moulder head is the granddaddy of all bristle and woven pad–backed sandpaper wheels. The bristles hold the sandpaper strips in contact with the workpiece. Backed sandpaper wheels such as this one are very good at working into surface intricacies and leave uniform finishes.

proper use of disc sanders involves working slowly and carefully. A 15-degree angle of the disc to the work is best. Your overlap and pass speed should be adjusted so that you never produce areas of blue metal, which is a sure sign of overheating the substrate.

Finally, there are two sanding devices that, for very different reasons, have limited application to automotive cleaning work. Hand-held belt sanders, with belts in the 3- to 4-inch-width range, are designed for sanding wood, particularly large flat items. They work well for that purpose. However, if you try to use them on metal, you find that they are bulky, awkward, and very prone to cutting serious grooves in vulnerable places. For items such as wooden tables, flat doors, and floor edges they are all but unbeatable. However, I have yet to find much good use for them in automotive metal cleaning work.

The second tool class that is not very useful for general automotive cleaning is the increasingly popular vibratory sander. These have some use in automotive work for sanding right up to the raised edges of items, including the flat areas around rivet heads. However, that job, and almost any other job that you can do with a vibratory sander, is often better accomplished with some other tool or process that is faster and less fussy. Vibratory sanders certainly work best on very small areas.

Many exotic and unusual abrasive-paper-based tools and systems have made their way to market and they often feature strange formats of abrasive papers. Among my least favorite are flap wheels and flails. Flails are almost useless for all but the most specialized operations

In the interesting but not very useful category (top, left-to-right): an abrasive pad and paper device and a sandpaper strip flail along with two flap wheels (bottom). Flap wheels don't accomplish anything that a disc sander, used properly, wouldn't accomplish, but they cost a lot more than plain sanding discs.

on very delicate items. Although flap wheels work, they tend to produce results similar to regular disc sanding at many times the cost of that simpler approach. Flap wheels can help you avoid overheating surfaces that might easily be burned with unskilled disc sanding approaches, but this kind of damage is also avoided by using a disc sander properly and carefully.

Abrasive Variables

In mechanically applied abrasive cleaning processes and procedures the main variables are abrasive media composition, backing composition, size, format on backing matrix, application motion pattern and pressure, speed of transit, angle of abrasive media to surface and to direction of transit, and dwell.

Media composition describes the substance on which the abrasive media is based. For example, abrasive papers can be based on materials such as aluminum oxide, garnet, silicon carbide, ceramic, flint sand, etc. Different media have different characteristics in terms of cost, durability, and effectiveness on the particular types of contamination and substrates you are sanding.

Abrasive media can be applied to paper, resinated paper, fabric, plastic sheet stock, fibrated mesh, and other materials. Some of these are waterproof and can be used for "wet sanding," while others cannot. Some may be cut into fine strips, or cut into specific shapes.

The particle size, or "grit," of abrasive media is critical. Larger grits work more quickly by gouging more deeply, while finer grits produce smoother finishes but tend to cut more slowly. Most sanding operations use multiple, escalating finer, grits to achieve smoother and finer finishes.

When you get into smaller grits, you may have a choice of media that are exactly sized to a specification, say 50, 80, 340, 400, 600, 2,000, or even 4,000 and beyond, as well as papers that average to a specification. Consistent media grit sizing is most common in the finer grits and makes for better results in fine sanding because you lessen the risk of contamination and scratching of your finish by larger particles in the mix. However, abrasive papers and cloths in this category, uniform grits, tend to be very expensive and are not really necessary for most sanding jobs.

Grits can be arranged in various densities on their backing materials. For example, some abrasive papers are described as "open grit," or "open coat," while others are "closed grit," or "closed coat." This distinction identifies how close individual particles of grit are to each other on a matrix. Closed grit papers tend to clog easily with spent abrasive and other sanding debris, while open grit papers do not clog as easily and last longer. When you are sanding something that is prone to clogging abrasive paper, such as rust or paint, the higher cost of open grit abrasives may be well worth the expenditure because it saves you time and some abrasive replacement costs.

The various remedies sold to cure or prevent clogging and to ease sanding motion, typically erasers and waxes, work to some extent. The good ones extend the life of abrasive papers in many cases, often significantly.

This brings us to the main operator-controlled variables in manual and machine sanding. These are refreshingly few: motion pattern, application pressure, speed of movement, angle of attack, and dwell.

Motion Pattern: Whether you are using a simple hand sanding pad or a power sander–driven flap wheel, your sanding pattern is critical to your results. This encompasses the machine's efficiency and quality. Straight-line patterns are the most basic approach. These can be repeated with various levels of overlap for each pass. Circular sanding patterns are also useful, particularly for blending the edges of sanded and unsanded areas. DA patterns combine random orbital motion with slow, circular motion and are very good for evenly scuffing surfaces or feather edging breaches in finishes. Many other patterns are both possible and useful, depending on what you are sanding and what you are trying to accomplish.

Application Pressure: Keeping the same three devices in mind (a sanding pad, a powered flap wheel, and a dual-action (DA) sander as well as any other hand-propelled or motor-driven device that comes to mind), consider the second variable: the pressure with which you apply the sanding media to a surface. It is critical. Too much pressure can burn the abrasive media and/or the surface you are sanding. Too little pressure

Bearing down too hard on this 8-inch DA sander to remove paint is inefficient. It's also slow, but very safe, with virtually no chance of burning into or cutting into metal excessively. However, its inefficiency renders it impractical.

A 7-inch disc sander with 50-grit abrasive is a fast and efficient way to remove old finishes and light rust from panels and/or whole cars. It takes skill and experience to use a disc sander safely and effectively. Note the correct 15-degree angle of the disc to the metal.

may result in skips and voids in your sanding. Experience should quickly inform you as to the best range of sanding pressures to use in various situations. As you sand, use your senses to note burning smells and the feeling of heat. Your eyes inform you of overheating areas by their color change. Also, you should be able to see if your sanding is consistent. The feel of the sander in your hands will also give you a sense of what is happening on a surface. Finally, the feel of the surface will inform you of your sanding progress.

Speed of Movement: The speed with which you move a sanding device along, or around, a surface correlates to the pressure you apply. At higher application pressures you need greater movement speed to avoid burning, while lower surface pressures allow slower movement speeds for the same reason. Again, be aware of these variables, and let experience be your guide in these matters.

Angle of Attack: Angle of attack applies to some power sanding operations and a few manual methods. For example, a disc sander is usually held at an ideal 15-degree contact angle to achieve the best results. On the other hand, jitterbug, DA, and inline sanders are almost always held flat to work, if the work is flat; they are rocked over the work, flat to the surface, if it is curved. Manual board sanders are often rocked over curved work and slid along and at an angle across it, but still held flat to it.

Dwell: Dwell relates to motion pattern, speed of motion, and application pressure, because it is dictated by all of them. Dwell is the specific amount of time that the abrasive surface is in contact with any particular place or area of the item that is being sanded. Dwell can be looked at as an instantaneous factor; it is the amount of time spent in contact with a particular place during each pass. Or it can be considered more generally as the total, aggregate amount of time spent on one place or area during sanding.

One particularly significant consideration with dwell occurs when using power sanding devices when the direction of the stroke is reversed. Dwell time inevitably increases at the segment where you change direction, if you don't take care to avoid this problem. This is similar to reversing the direction of a spray gun for a return pass. In both cases, you should take steps to avoid excessive dwell at the points of reversal. Triggering or lifting your power sanding device helps accomplish this, as does increasing speed across the surface when you reverse direction.

In the case of instantaneous dwell, take into account factors such as local burning by the abrasive, or removing a high spot from a surface by spending slightly more time abrading it. As a general consideration, dwell can be a factor in trying to average the height or texture of one area that you are sanding into another when these areas have slightly different histories and different surface profiles and characteristics.

The most important thing to note is that each type of sanding media and device has its own rules covering the variables of movement pattern, application pressure, movement speed, angle of attack, and dwell. These variables reappear in many other cleaning situations, from abrasive blasting to mechanical media applications and processes.

Other Mechanical Abrasives, Devices and Processes

The list of mechanical media types and devices is all but endless. I keep discovering additions to it as

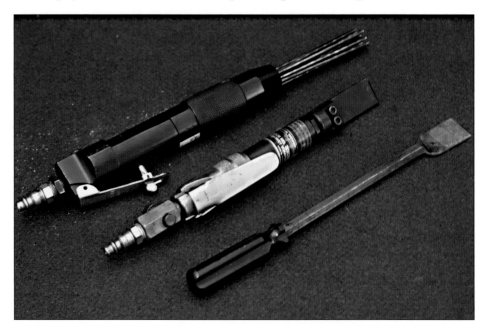

Top to bottom: A needle scaler, an air-powered scraper, and a hand scraper. The needle scaler works well on intricate areas in castings. The power scraper is great for removing stubborn deposits from large, flat surfaces. The hand scraper is the weapon of first resort in any grime removal situation.

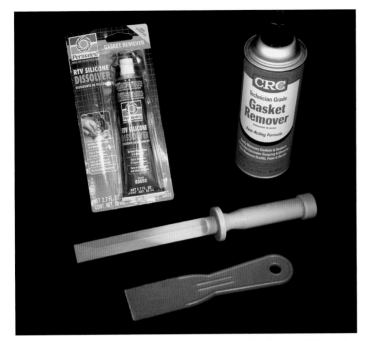

Some surfaces are just too soft and fragile for traditional scraping approaches. CRC Gasket Remover softens most gasket compounds. Permatex RTV silicone dissolver does wonders softening silicone rubber gasket residues. Using the plastic scrapers below them is a good way to pamper aluminum and plastic flange surfaces.

Poly mesh and nylon bristle finishing wheels are among the newer cleaning methods that have become widely available recently. For many years, these wheels were available only to industry professionals. They are available in many compositions and include many kinds of abrasive loads.

With an aggressive abrasive such as aluminum oxide, this rock polisher–type tumbler can effectively clean items such as these small fasteners. It's slow, but works nicely for small parts batches that can be cleaned at leisure before they are needed.

I go along. A few of my favorites are hand scrapers, power scrapers, and needle scalers. These are particularly useful for dealing with several very specific situations. Hand scrapers are the best choice to clean gasketed flanges easily, a very common procedure in many mechanical repair and restoration jobs.

Power scrapers are often useful when large flat mating surfaces must be cleansed of stubborn soils. It should be noted that there are some situations for which neither of these tools, or any sharp-edged metal tool, should be used because they may gouge delicate surfaces, such as plastic and aluminum flanges. In these situations, use chemical cleaners in combination with very soft, finely bristled wire brushes, plastic cleaning meshes and/or scrapers, or abrasive papers.

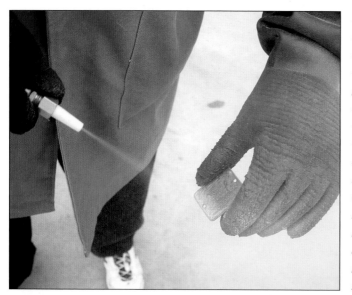

New processes and new blasting media keep adding to the already enormous possibilities of media blasting for cleaning metal. This one, bicarbonate of soda blasting, has been around for a couple of decades but is now coming into general use as knowledge of its capabilities has spread.

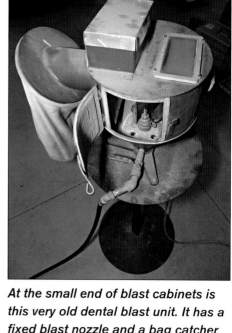

At the small end of blast cabinets is this very old dental blast unit. It has a fixed blast nozzle and a bag catcher for debris and spent abrasive. It was once used to clean small dental castings and remains useful for cleaning small parts, such as automotive fasteners.

Open-air blasting situations, such as this one, don't allow for easy media recovery and reuse. They are sometimes used for blasting large projects, including entire cars. They are also useful for blasting smaller objects, such as this hood side panel, where the item size exceeds the size of an available blast cabinet.

This industrial cabinet is about average in size and was state of the art three or four decades ago. Used commercial blast cabinets can be found frequently at highly favorable prices. They are often a better alternative than buying consumer-grade equipment that lacks industrial durability.

Also recommended for mechanically removing surface contamination from soft materials are nylon bristled wheels, Scotch-Brite–type plastic mesh wheels, and poly wheels. Cotton or sisal polishing wheels are effective, too, as are tumbling and vibratory cleaning treatments. The list is almost endless.

Blast Cleaning Systems

Blast cleaning systems are among the most efficient and effective ways to clean metal.

I suppose that the concept for abrasive blasting was borne on desert winds such as the Saharan siroccos, sand-laden winds that bombarded northern Africa and southern Europe long before the beginning of human history, and ever since. Libyans, Spaniards, and many others must have noted the destructive and erosive effects of those blasts on natural and manmade artifacts and structures.

Humans got into the sandblasting act as early as 1870 with the invention of air compressors that could propel abrasives in air streams at high speeds. Patents were issued. By the turn of the 20th Century, practical sandblasting equipment was available and abrasive blasting developed into a very useful technology. Its development has continued at a rapid pace.

Blasting equipment and systems vary greatly in size and features. Some are contained in cubic-foot cabinets while some blasting rooms are large enough to hold trucks and large equipment. Most contained blasting systems are between these two size extremes.

Blast systems either recycle their abrasives or disperse them in the environment. Most, but not all,

This is the simplest kind of siphon-type blast system. Spent media and contamination fall to the bottom of the cabinet, into a hopper, and then into a T-fitting that replaces the hopper's original output port. From there, it is pulled up the hose on the right, into a siphon gun.

contained systems employ recycling provisions. Soda blasting is the most prominent exception. Recycling systems either sort used abrasive into sound abrasive and refuse, or present unsorted abrasive and blasting debris together for reuse.

Systems that sort recycled material are usually pressure systems. Systems that do not sort used abrasives are almost always siphon systems. This distinction has to do with abrasives being delivered to the blasting air stream either under pressure or by siphon action.

Siphon Blaster

Siphon blasters use a Bernoulli effect partial vacuum to raise abrasive media and air into a blasting gun, and then accelerate the media

in the air stream that created the partial vacuum that raised it. Its main advantages are that it's a simple system with no moving parts and it is comparatively inexpensive to build. The entire siphon delivery system is contained in a hopper containing abrasive media and a hose that connects the hopper to a blast gun. The gun siphons and releases the media at high speed. The great disadvantage of siphon systems is that they are inefficient compared to pressure systems. In fact, up to 80 percent of the air energy consumed by siphon systems is used to raise the media into the gun. That leaves a mere 20 percent of that energy to accelerate the media toward its target. Siphon systems also allow very little adjustment of the air-to-media mix ratio.

Air blows over this siphon gun's internal port, creating suction in the hose to the right. That raises and feeds abrasive and air into the gun from which it is propelled. Roughly 75 percent of the compressed air energy in this system is used to move abrasive into the gun.

A pressure nozzle is much simpler than the siphon nozzle shown above. It is fed a controlled mixture of air and abrasive media under pressure. It is four or five times more efficient than a siphon gun in its use of compressed air.

Recycling Pressure

Approaching 100-percent efficiency, pressure systems are much more effective at transferring compressed air energy into the actual blast process. They are also complex, expensive, and, often, finicky to maintain.

In recycling pressure systems, the media is delivered to a holding tank mounted over a pressure pot. When the system is triggered, a valve that connects the holding tank to the top of the pressure pot closes the pressure pot; then, another valve allows air pressure into the pot. Air pressure and gravity force media out of the bottom of the pot, through a manual mixing valve, and then into a compressed air stream (through a hose) to the system's discharge nozzle. Both the media and air stream can be valved for an optimum mix of media and blast air.

When the system operator closes the system actuating valve, air pressure in the blast output reduces to zero, as the blast nozzle releases residual pressure in the system. Then, the valve on top of the pressure pot opens, and the sorted media stored in the abrasive tank above it falls into the pressure pot for the next operating cycle. These sequences require several valves. In addition, the metering valve for the media is subject to considerable wear by the pressurized abrasives that flow through it. All of the valves and controls involved in this sequence can require considerable maintenance.

As noted, pressure systems usually employ a method of separating the used abrasives and blasting debris from the good abrasive, the latter for recycling back into the system. A blast cabinet usually accomplishes this with a fan that pulls the spent abrasive out of the blast area and delivers it to a cyclone (spiral) chamber. As it whirs around in that chamber, the lighter materials, spent abrasive, and blasted debris that have become dust, are pushed out of a port at the periphery of the spiral motion and into a dust collector bag or cabinet for removal. The heavier, intact media is too heavy to be pushed out of the cyclone chamber and slides down a ramp surface to a hole in the center of the cyclone chamber, ending up in the holding tank above the pressure pot.

When the pot is depressurized at the end of its blasting cycle, sound media falls into it and is recycled, becoming active media when the tank is re-pressurized.

Siphon systems may include a cyclone separator, but many do not. If they do not, the spent abrasive and the broken media and blasting debris are delivered to the gun for reuse. This is less than optimal.

Clearly, pressurized systems with separation are superior in efficiency and result quality when compared to siphon systems, especially if a siphon system does not have media separation. But pressure systems (particularly those with separation) are much more complex and expensive than siphon systems (especially those without separation). The

Here is an entire open-air siphon blasting system. It's crude, inefficient, cheap, and very useful for occasionally blasting small parts. Note that it is fitted with a much better siphon gun than usually comes with these inexpensive units.

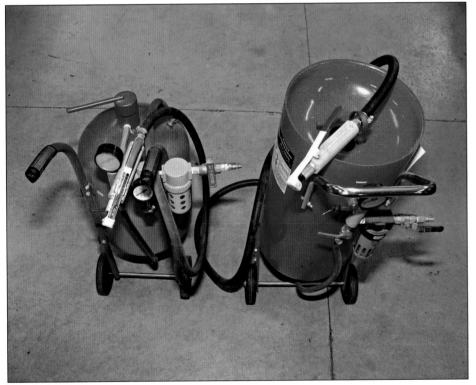

Pressure blasting outfits such as these can be bought for $100 or less and are very usable and reasonably durable, up to a point. Don't expect them to withstand commercial duty, and plan to refill them with media often because they do not recycle it automatically.

differences can be between fifty and several thousand dollars. The cheaper systems work, but are slow and inefficient compared to the better pressure systems with separation. They also require much more air, and therefore larger compressors, to achieve the blast performance of a full pressure system.

Peening Media

Not all blast cleaning is done with air delivery media systems. Some cleaning operations involve the use of peening media in mechanically generating systems. These are often found in industry, and in the auto reconditioning sector. They are intended to deal with items such as cast-iron cylinder blocks, heads, valves, crankshafts, etc., and are commonly seen where production rebuilding of parts like cast-iron water pumps and master and wheel cylinders is performed.

These cleaning systems are usually automated or semi-automated because they involve several stages. They use peening media and not cutting media. The first stage in this sequence is to oven bake the parts being cleaned to incinerate and loosen carbon deposits, paint, and rust. Next, they are placed in a cabinet and subjected to the high-speed attack of randomly generated untargeted, peening media, such as large steel shot. This media cleans by pounding surface material loose. Peening media is round and does not cut the base metal; it just smashes baked and rusted debris into submission.

It should be noted that many varieties of peening media are available, not just steel shot. For example, glass bead is another peening media that works by impact, rather than by cutting. After some number of passes, or "cycles," through the blasting process, glass bead characteristically disintegrates into fine dust that is removed easily by a cyclone separator. It should not turn into sharp fragments that can cut metal. Steel shot does not fragment, but it does go out-of-round, at which point it should be replaced.

Wet Blasting

Finally, there is a new kid on the block in abrasive media delivery systems: wet blasting. Well, it isn't exactly new, but rather reinvented and remarketed. Wet blasting involves spraying out a cutting media, such as sand or glass shards, accompanied by water vapor.

Although this kind of equipment has been available for decades under such names as vapor blasting and slurry blasting, it was reintroduced recently by two companies in new, more affordable systems that are said to require much less maintenance than the older wet-blast systems.

These companies claim that the new wet-blasting processes are economical, fast, and suitable for blasting auto body sheet metal without producing the distortion and warping that can accompany some traditional blasting formats. However, questions arise about how to prevent water from becoming trapped in the intricacies of auto bodies, where it can cause rusting from the inside out. And while the media to run these machines (typically fractured bottle glass) is relatively inexpensive, the equipment for this process is definitely quite expensive. I present some conclusions regarding wet blasting later in this book.

Media Types

It is almost safe to say that if you can think of a substance, any substance, someone has probably tried to use it as a blasting medium. In the 150-year history of abrasive blasting, hundreds, maybe thousands, of materials have been tried. Four basic distinctions separate these blasting media: hardness, particle shape, breakdown modes, and particle size.

They may be soft or hard, depending on their intended purpose. Hardness is gauged on the Rockwell or, more often, the Mohs hardness scale, which runs from 1 (talc) to 10 (diamond). Well-known blasting abrasives, such as aluminum oxide and silicon carbide, are in the 9 to 10 range, while bicarbonate of

This is the business end of a commercial shot-peening machine. Two 5-hp motors drive centrifugal wheels that shoot random blasts of steel shot into and around the cabinet above them. This is a thorough and efficient way to clean parts, but the equipment costs thousands of dollars.

Blast media manufacturers and suppliers love to provide material samples such as those shown here. On the left is plastic media and on the right is steel shot in various sizes. Although you can't tell much about media performance by simply looking at media, it's interesting to see what you are using.

soda and calcium carbonate (chalk) are in the 2 to 3 range.

Agricultural media, such as corncobs, pulverized walnut shells, apricot pits, and many others, tend to be at the soft end of the scale, in the 1 to 5 range. Manmade media, such as Plastic Media Blasting (PMB) and urea, are among designer abrasives that are also found all over the lower ranges of the Mohs scale.

Blast media can also be characterized by particle shape. Some, such as aluminum oxide and silicone carbide, are sharp and tend to cut aggressively. They are also hard. Others such as glass bead, are round and dull and tend to peen rather than cut. Soft agricultural media tend to polish, rather than cut and clean.

It is also useful to consider the breakdown modes of blasting media. Some, such as bicarb, are good for only one pass before they shatter into dust. Others, such as glass bead, remain round and flexible until multiple trips and impacts fatigue and harden them to the point that they lose their resilience and break down into dust. This tends to happen suddenly and completely for each glass sphere.

Some media (again, such as glass bead) break down cleanly into an easily removed dust, while others, such as chilled copper slag, produce smudging dark residues.

A final consideration is media particle size. This is often measured as a mesh or screen size, the number of holes per inch in a standard mesh measuring screen through which a particular size of media falls. The mesh number includes the thickness of the screen dividers, so the particle pass size is a bit less than the mesh number would seem to indicate. For example, a 10 mesh passes particles up to .787 inch, not .10 inch as you might expect. All common blasting media fit into a screen mesh range of 4 to 325, with both ends of that mesh range being extremes of particle size.

Other designating systems for media size include the ought system, that is, 0, 00, 000, and 0000, to designate increasing fineness. Some manufacturers use letter designations or words (e.g., "fine," "medium," and "coarse").

Other considerations may influence media choices, but the basics of hardness, shape, breakdown mode, and size are foremost.

Blast System Variables

Most blasting for cleaning purposes is accomplished with air-generated media, so this book concentrates on that blasting method. The learning curve for operating these systems is relatively mild in slope, but

Mixing valves are the heart of all pressure blasting systems. This foot operable crank valve adjusts the air/media ratio. Blast media enters the T-fitting below the mixing valve and joins the air stream that arrives from the right. The mixed air and abrasive exit via the hose on the left.

Optimizing the blast angle can improve work efficiency, but it is not always worth the effort. In the case of this part, the surfaces are too small to bother much with blast angle. Any angle gets the job done before you can change it to one that, theoretically, might be better.

long in time. You can grasp the basics of how to use air-generated blasting technology very quickly, and continue to perfect your technique for different media and substrates for the rest of your life.

The basic considerations are blast media type and mesh size, air pressure, nozzle pass speed and dwell on any point(s), nozzle distance to target, nozzle angle, and media density (finely controllable in pressure systems only). It takes keen observation and analytical effort to optimize all of these factors.

In most cases, blast pressures run between 40 and 120 psi. You have to set pressure at a level that is efficient, but not destructive to what you are blasting. To a great extent, this depends on the other factors already mentioned. Still, blast pressure and nozzle size are the most basic factors that you control in abrasive blasting.

Nozzle pass speed and dwell also depend on the other variable factors. For example, if pressures are too high, or nozzle pass speeds are too low, you run the risk of warping thin sections of metal, such as auto body panels. With delicate substrates, you risk cutting right through them. However, if these factors are set too low, you spend an unnecessary amount of time completing jobs. Different target distances and attack angles greatly influence what pressure works best.

The distance from the nozzle to the target also relates to the other factors. With higher pressures you may need to use a greater distances to avoid warping substrates with some media, but you get a broader blast patterns on the targets.

In most cases, nozzle angle is not directly related to the other blasting factors. The standard starting nozzle-to-work angle is 45 degrees, but that is just a starting point. The actual physics of nozzle angle are daunting, but adjustment by trial-and-error becomes a relatively simple matter. Different jobs benefit from different nozzle angles. Some coatings can be undercut with very narrow angles; narrow in the sense of being relatively parallel to the blasted target.

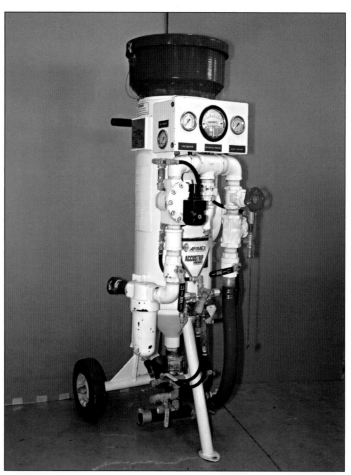

This high-end soda-blasting pressure pot allows its operator to gain fine control of many blasting variables. That's great for production blasting, but not really necessary for most automotive shop work. Even so, this kind of control can be very educational in terms of how blast variables relate to specific outcomes and results.

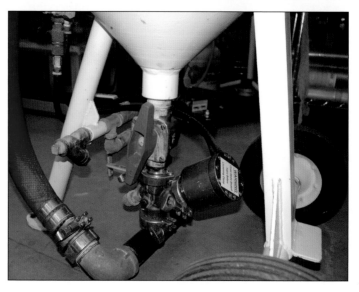

The heart of this pot's system is its Thompson Valve (shown). It allows very fine and consistent control of the blast air/media mix. If you need very consistent results, this is one way to achieve them in your blast stream.

Rust, on the other hand, may yield most quickly to fairly perpendicular blast angles. That is because coating and rust removal rely on three basic factors: undercutting, stretching, and surface erosion. These three factors come into play in varying proportions depending on the combinations and conditions of the coatings and substrates involved. Likewise, different media may take advantage of them in different ways.

Pressure blast systems, as opposed to siphon systems, allow pretty fine adjustment of blast density, the amount of media in the blasting air stream. Both very high media and very low media densities tend to slow the blasting process, all other variables being equal. Very high densities also tend to block your view of what is happening on the blast surface, depending on the intensity of your air removal system.

Let's look at the removal factors separately. Undercutting may work at 45 degrees but often works even better at lesser angles, depending on the other variables, such as pressure and gun distance. That is because, as the name implies, undercutting directly deteriorates the bonds that attach a coating or contaminant to a substrate.

Stretching works by literally expanding a coating's outer surface with impact, until the bonds underneath it break through stretching. This frequently works best at angles between 45 and 90 degrees; again, depending on the other blasting variables and on the coating composition and level of adhesion.

In the case of some very hard or resilient coatings and contaminants, removal is mostly accomplished by eroding ("sanding") the coating or contaminant away from the substrate, from its outermost surface to its innermost layer. This tends to be the slowest and most difficult mode of removal.

Most situations use all three removal modes in varying combinations. Sequences and modes vary, but these are the basic ways to understand how blasting cleans metal. The important issue is that, with keen observation and sound analysis, you can make pretty good guesses at how a coating or contaminant is being removed and adjust the blasting variables under your control to best use the operative factors.

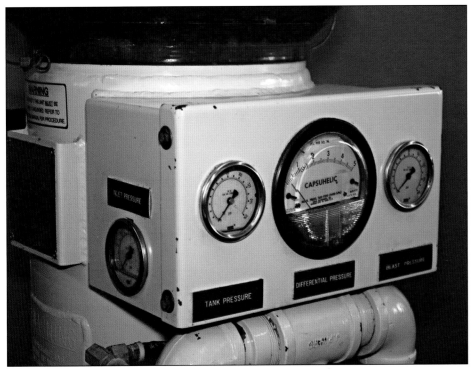

The dashboard on this high-end blast pot has four telemetry functions. It shows incoming air pressure, pot pressure, blast hose pressure, and (center gauge) the difference between the last two items. All good stuff, if you need to know it. In most situations you don't.

To put it politely, someone got blast-happy cleaning these hubcaps. Attempting to clean them up with blasting, he or she cut through the surfaces of two of them and added to the damage on several others. This is an extreme case of not having the blast variables under control.

ALTERNATIVE APPROACHES TO CLEANING METAL

This chapter considers some of the less common approaches to cleaning metal. These approaches are not inferior to the more common approaches, nor are they necessarily more difficult to access or use. Rather, they are out of the mainstream because they require complex and expensive equipment, pose safety or environmental concerns, or are used primarily in industry. They are also processes that, for various reasons, often find their best uses when employed in conjunction with other processes. In many cases, they are optional pre-cleaning steps for mainstream cleaning, and in turn, they often increase the overall efficiency or quality of those processes.

Because alternative approaches exist, and because, in some special situations, they are superior to standard processes when they either replace or supplement them, they are worth discussing here.

Steam and Pressure Washing

Of all of the substances on Earth, water is closest to being "the universal solvent." Yes, good old water, aqua marine, H_2O, etc., dissolves more earthly substances than any other known element or chemical compound. Because water is common, benevolent, and necessary to sustain life, it seems unlikely that it would be an aggressive cleaning solvent, but it is.

"Well, what about this acid or that corrosive?" you might ask. "It'll

What you see here isn't really steam cleaning. Actual steam cleaning isn't nearly as dramatic. Here, a steam cleaner has been set to deliver very hot water vapor. With real steam, you wouldn't see anything until the steam cooled to pressurized water vapor, which is what you see here.

This small electric pressure washer is capable of 1,400 psi and comes with a high-pressure detergent injector (not shown). Units such as this are inexpensive, portable, and useful for small jobs. They lack the serious cleaning power and the durability required to remove bad soils or to do large jobs.

This $4,000 monster is a serious steam cleaner that can operate continuously, while producing high-volume steam. Its Honda 388-cc engine runs on gasoline, while its boiler consumes kerosene, diesel, or fuel oil. It produces hot pressurized water, or steam, up to 250 degrees F and pumps up to 4 gpm at 3,000 psi. (Photo Courtesy of Northern Tools & Equipment)

eat through most metals as if they were cheese."

Maybe so, but when looked at in the context of all of the materials on Earth, liquids other than water are found to be less solvent on more substances than good old water.

There was an old joke about a farm family whose son was the first ever to attend college. When he came home from Good Ol' State for Christmas his first year he was quizzed by his dad regarding what he was learning at the state university. He said that chemistry was his major and that most of his classes were in chemistry. His dad asked him what he was learning in chemistry. The son responded, "Well, we're looking for the universal solvent, something that dissolves everything."

His dad asked, "What're you gonna keep it in when you find it?" You might want to keep that in mind the next time you take a drink of water because, as I said, it's closer to being the universal solvent than anything else on Earth.

The astounding solvency of water is due to its molecule's bipolar nature, which exposes strongly active and relatively unshielded hydrogen atoms. Water's solvency is fully realized under three conditions:

1. When it is produced and delivered in a sub-particulate size; that is, a size smaller than its smallest droplet format, such as in a spray or vapor. In this condition, water's solvency is greatly increased because it is not constrained by surface tension. In liquid form, the surface tension restrains its chemically active nature at the surface by locking its molecules to each other, which makes it less solvent.

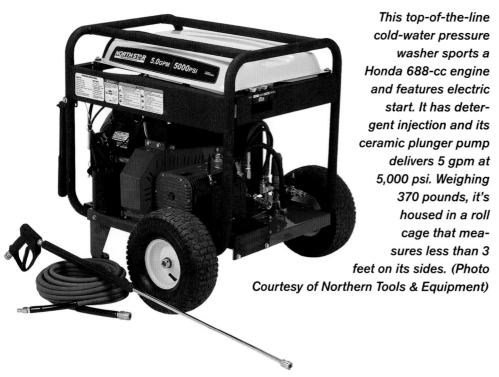

This top-of-the-line cold-water pressure washer sports a Honda 688-cc engine and features electric start. It has detergent injection and its ceramic plunger pump delivers 5 gpm at 5,000 psi. Weighing 370 pounds, it's housed in a roll cage that measures less than 3 feet on its sides. (Photo Courtesy of Northern Tools & Equipment)

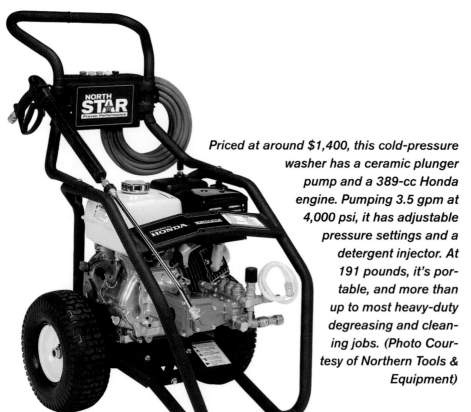

Priced at around $1,400, this cold-pressure washer has a ceramic plunger pump and a 389-cc Honda engine. Pumping 3.5 gpm at 4,000 psi, it has adjustable pressure settings and a detergent injector. At 191 pounds, it's portable, and more than up to most heavy-duty degreasing and cleaning jobs. (Photo Courtesy of Northern Tools & Equipment)

2. When its temperature is elevated, particularly at, near, or above, 212 degrees F (at sea level), the point at and beyond which water turns into a vapor, steam, or fine mist condensate. In the case of steam (known as a "phase change" in water), water is automatically converted into a sub-particulate format as a result of being at very high energy levels. That is one reason why steam is a far more effective solvent than water in its liquid format, particularly as a very cold liquid. Of course, water's other common phase change is into a solid, that is, ice. Ice has very limited solvent properties, but it does have some abrasive potential.

3. The third condition that enhances the solvency of water is when it is delivered at high velocity toward a target.

Another reason for water's greatly enhanced high-temperature solvency is that heated water molecules have more energy to attack things. The hotter they are, the fiercer they become. Moreover, this aggressiveness is even further enhanced at high velocities.

Contrary to popular belief, steam is not the stuff that you see coming out of the spout on a boiling kettle, or for that matter, being emitted by most steam cleaners. Steam is a gas that is invisible to the human eye. What you see exiting that kettle's spout is condensed steam (water vapor), albeit very hot water vapor. Any steam that is present is invisible. If half an inch, or an inch, of *nothing* is visible between the spout's end and the foggy stuff that it is visibly emitting under pressure, that space is real, live steam. The foggy stuff beyond it is condensed water vapor, the stuff of which clouds are made. The water vapor may be very hot and very solvent, but it isn't steam.

This distinction is important, because in a practical sense real steam results from heating water above its boiling point of 212 degrees F (at sea level). To do useful work such as driving a steam engine or running a steam cleaner the temperature of water must reach 300 degrees F or higher. Of course, at temperatures above boiling water goes into its gaseous phase and exerts expansive pressure.

If, for example, you raise water to a temperature of 300 degrees F in a containment vessel, it exerts a pressure of 67 psi. By 400 degrees F you are getting 250 psi, which may not sound like much, but it is just about in the top of the range of pressures at which steam locomotives once operated.

Steam cleaners typically operate at a range of 0 to 150 psi, usually below the middle of that range. This sounds puny when compared to the thousands of pounds that some pressure washers deliver, but is plenty of pressure for many cleaning jobs. Remember, steam relies on factors other than pressure to achieve its terrific cleaning power. The solvency of highly energized and dissociated water molecules is the key to those other factors.

A real steam cleaner, one capable of producing real steam in useful quantities, is an expensive, complex, and somewhat dangerous rig. Steam can inflict terrible burns, and there is no way to see steam that is coming in your direction. Most steam cleaners can be, and are, run as very hot water pressure washers. After all, hot water vapor is a far better solvent than the cold water vapor that issues

from some low-end gas and electric pressure washers.

As with that boiling kettle that I mentioned, if you can see a misty discharge coming out of a steam cleaner's nozzle, it is water vapor that is cooler than steam. It may be very hot, but cooler than steam. Any space between the end of the nozzle and visible vapor is occupied by real, live steam.

In most cases, real steam cleaners are complex and expensive pieces of industrial equipment. Unless you are regularly cleaning a lot of very grungy items, or need to sanitize the walls and machinery in a food factory, they are unnecessary.

Lighter-duty steam cleaners still have boilers and pumps to add water to their pressurized steam vessels, but they are often used as high-pressure washers with the capability of raising the temperature of cold water to high levels. These machines are still expensive and complex, but they can be very useful for continuous and/or occasional use. They are often adjusted to produce very light steam at their discharge nozzles. However, they basically produce very hot streams of condensing water vapor with considerable force behind them at the points that they reach the items to be cleaned. Although this lacks the full cleaning power of steam, it's a lot safer and results in a very credible water solvent system for removing heavy grease, oil, tar, and other soils that are softened by heat. High-temperature pressure washers become particularly effective when detergent is added to their discharges.

Industrial Processes

The list of exotic and off-the-beaten-track methods of cleaning

Adequate for most basic cold pressure washing jobs, this small gas-powered unit pumps 2.5 gpm at 3,000 psi. It has a 208-cc OHV gasoline engine and detergent injection. At 70 pounds, it's portable, and generally useful for performing automotive tasks such as degreasing and blowing off loose mud, rust, and paint. (Photo Courtesy of Northern Tools & Equipment)

metal is long. Some of these have very specific applications, such as cleaning electrical circuit board conductors or NASA vehicle components for use, or reuse, in space. Most such processes are task-specific and are defined to incredibly precise and difficult to attain specifications. These are most usually described as "industrial" or "scientific" cleaning processes.

The central fact about unusual and exotic processes is that sometimes they become mainstream as their underlying technology matures. Some cleaning equipment and techniques that were once exotic, and pretty much beyond the reach of individuals and small enterprises, are now commonplace in those realms.

Pressure washing and abrasive blasting fit that description.

For that reason I mention and briefly describe a few industrial cleaning processes that are presently generally unavailable to most of us, at least in forms that perform well, but that may become much more common in coming years. If you don't believe that this really can happen, consider once-exotic equipment, such as arc welders and, later, MIG welders. These were once the exclusive province of enterprises such as the Big-Three car companies but are now common in small commercial shops and even in homeowners' workshops. Or ponder plasma arc metal cutters that, a few decades ago, were beyond the reach of anyone

not actively engaged in some aspect of the steel industry. They are now compact and inexpensive enough for almost anyone to own.

Soda Blasting

Soda blasting is covered in Chapter 5 as a distinct type of abrasive blasting. I think that soda blasting is one of the most under-appreciated and misunderstood cleaning processes available. Its potential is far greater than most people realize, and I strongly suspect that it may be the next "big thing" in automotive abrasive cleaning.

That said, truly effective soda-blasting equipment is still far too expensive for most automotive repair, restoration, or custom situations. This may sound a bit odd, since consumer

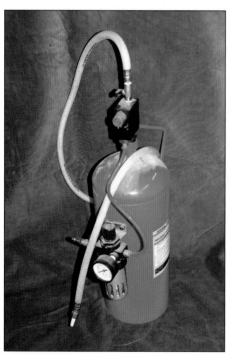

This inexpensive soda pressure blasting pot can be very useful for many small cleaning jobs. Although it packs great value for what you get, it's not economical to operate because it consumes an unnecessarily large amount of soda. For occasional use it can be a handy item to have.

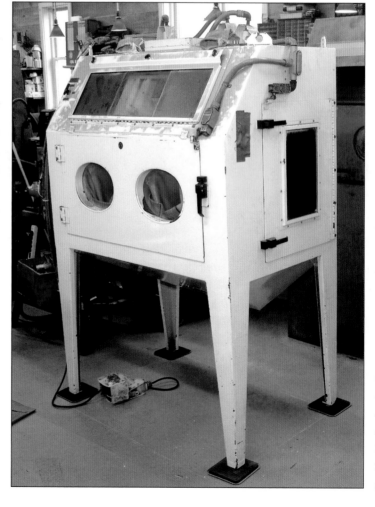

This Ruemelin soda-blasting cabinet is state-of-the-art in every way. One of its unique features is a system that allows the operator to see clearly through what is usually the fog of soda blasting. It is also a heavy-duty and durable unit that is designed for production blasting.

versions of soda-blasting pressure pots are widely advertised and well known to be broadly available in the $100 to $800 range, with bicarbonate of soda selling for between $7 and $40 for a 40- or 50-pound bag, *not including shipping*. That shipping, by the way, can cost half, or more, of the cost of the 50-pound bag of high-quality soda. And, in most applications, it takes a lot of soda to blast paint off a part. In addition, remember that soda is only good for one trip through a blaster. It is not reusable.

You should also consider the fact that inexpensive soda-blasting equipment is often extremely inefficient. It can consume as much as four times the amount of soda that quality equipment would use to do the same job. Better-quality machines will do better work.

The great advantage of soda blasting is that it creates no discernable or (in the real world) measurable dimensional change in metal. Depending on particle size and blast pressure, it can be used on glass and most metallic trim without damaging their surfaces. It has been shown to be extremely effective at eradicating legendarily difficult-to-remove finishes, such as epoxy paints and powder coating. It is also environmentally neutral, requiring no heroic efforts to keep its residues from polluting sites where it is used.

Soda blasting carries two main drawbacks for use in automotive stripping. At 2.8 on the Mohs hardness scale, soda is not an aggressive blast media, and it certainly is not capable of removing deep, pitting rust. It removes light surface rust and rust scale.

Because it does not alter metal surfaces dimensionally, soda blasting does not leave a desirable "tooth"

profile (or "anchor" pattern) on metal surfaces to promote mechanical adhesion of primers and paints. However, use of "reactive primers" (etching primers) obviates that need to a great extent.

Soda blasting is certainly a serious contender. I predict that it will be used in an increasing number of automotive applications in the years to come.

Wet Blasting

Wet blasting has been around in one form or another for decades. The basic concept is to either add water to an abrasive blast at or near its point of discharge, or to blast both materials in the same stream from a common source, such as the same pressure pot. In this second example, water and abrasive are pressurized in a pressure pot and delivered together from a single hose and nozzle in the form of solid blast media and water vapor. This approach has recently achieved a great deal of publicity in systems delivered by Dustless Blasting (a division of MMLJ).

Originally, this method was employed in cabinets and carried names such as slurry blasting, vapor blasting, liquid honing, and others. More recently, portable wet-blasting outfits have reached the market. The equipment now being sold for wet blasting comes in a wide variety of designs, but all of it is intrinsically complex and quite expensive. Wet-blasting abrasives vary from traditional media such as garnet, aluminum oxide, and flint sands, to new abrasives such as fractured bottle glass.

The claimed advantages of wet blasting as it applies to automotive use, and particularly sheet-metal parts, are that it removes everything,

including rust, and that it does not warp metal. It is also said to be comparatively non-destructive to some trim parts, and it is claimed that wet blasting is easily defeated with simple masking measures. Some wet-blasting equipment vendor videos show impressive coating removal rates along with the lack of dimensional and warping damage. At the very least, wet blasting combines the inherent solvency of sub-particulate water with the aggressiveness of the various solid media with which it is combined.

Reservations about wet blasting abound. The primary concern is the complete removal of moisture from complex structures, such as auto bodies, after they are soaked by the wet-blasting process. If moisture remains in the intricacies of the bodies, and then under subsequently applied paint that may trap it, it can fester into rust. Questions remain about the long-term effectiveness of using rust-preventing additives in after-blast rinses to retard or eliminate post-blast rusting. Some of the individuals and companies selling wet-blasting equipment dismiss these issues as non-existent. Most sheet-metal experts whom I know tend to take these matters very seriously.

I think that wet-blasting technology has considerable future potential, but I remain unconvinced that it is ready for prime time in its present state. Its application to cleaning architectural artifacts, such as masonry, makes sense, but in the present state of its development its use in stripping automobile bodies raises too many unanswered questions for me to recommend it. In a few years we will all know a lot more about this new process because we

Cryo Blasting

All photos in this sidebar are courtesy of TuneRS Mall.

TuneRS Mall of Pompano Beach, Florida, is a Porsche restoration and preservation shop. It offers CryoDetail, a service that employs dry ice blasting for the purpose of detailing high-end collectable cars. The results are impressive. The shop was kind enough to supply a variety of photographs of its unusual CryoDetail cleaning process. These before-and-after photos demonstrate the capabilities of dry ice blasting for automobile detailing and restoration.

Cryo blasting, or dry ice blasting, is another technology that has been around for decades in various states of development. The equipment to accomplish it is relatively complex and expensive, and its use is limited to a small number of situations. However, it excels in those situations.

This method uses frozen CO_2 (carbon dioxide), also called dry ice, as its

Removing undercoating is just one of the many capabilities of dry ice blasting. This photo from TuneRS Mall of its CryoDetail process shows half of the undercoating stripped from a 1961 Mercedes Benz fuel tank. Dry ice blasting accomplished this usually messy job quickly and cleanly by any standard.

These photos show the general capability of the TuneRS Mall CryoDetail system to remove grease, dirt, and grunge from the mechanical parts of this Ferrari 328 GTB. This was accomplished in a matter of minutes, but probably would take much longer with any other process.

blasting media in particle sizes that are typically about the size of a grain of rice. Blast pressures are between 30 and 100 psi. Of course, to use cryo blasting you need a source of delivered dry ice particles of the correct size.

Dry ice as a blasting media offers several advantages. Like bicarbonate of soda, it doesn't harm or change the dimensions of a blast target. It doesn't even leave residue because its life after blasting is to return to its gaseous form and rejoin the atmosphere. Although cryo blasting is best suited to uses in manufacturing enterprises, such as food and pharmaceuticals, it is also useful for detailing cars and parts, where it removes loose corrosion, oil, grease, loose paint, dirt, and other lightly adhering contaminants. It also cleans rubber and plastic parts without damaging them. ■

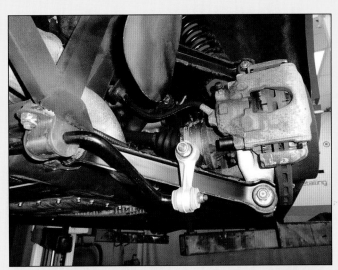

Here you see the strengths and limits of dry ice blasting. It does a great job of removing grease, undercoating, and flying smut, but it cannot remove rust or other forms of deep, strongly adhered contamination from this Ferrari 328 GTB brake and undercarriage area.

Taken from different angles, these before-and-after suspension and undercarriage photographs of a Porsche 993 Turbo show the ability of dry ice blasting to remove most of the surface effects of a fire. I know of no other way to accomplish this as completely, quickly, and economically.

Cryo Blasting *CONTINUED*

A closer look at the lower control arm and tie rod area of the burned Porsche 993 indicates how clean the alloy and other parts are after dry ice blasting.

Here you see the CryoDetail process applied to a wider area of a burned Porsche 993 Turbo and to a variety of different surfaces. In every area, it produces an improvement. Approaching this job with steam cleaning or solvent and a brush would take longer and produce a lesser result. It would also risk water contamination of delicate surfaces and mechanical areas.

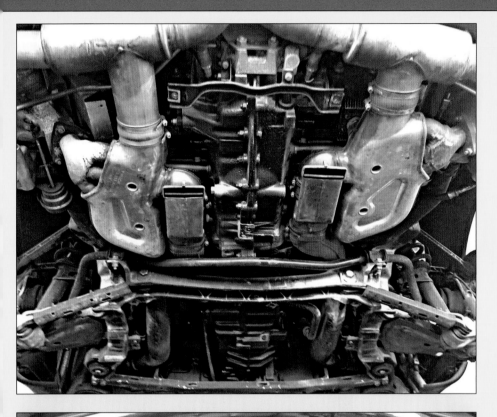

These photos of the burned Porsche 993 Turbo again show the ability of dry ice blasting to rejuvenate many different kinds and compositions of surfaces, and to remove a wide variety of contaminants, such as undercoating, road grime, and the effects of a fire.

Cryo Blasting *CONTINUED*

The top two photographs are of the underside of the engine, exhaust, and shocks of a 1991 Ferrari Testarossa. The bottom two photographs show the results of the application of the CryoDetail process. The results are dramatic and speak for themselves.

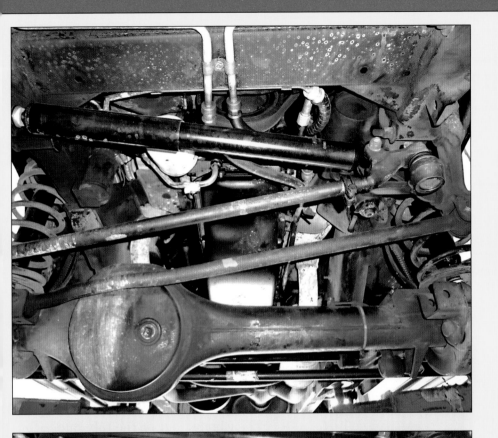

The before-and-after photographs of this 1997 Land Rover rear axle area demonstrate the use of dry ice blasting to do general cleanup of an undercarriage. The improvement is impressive, while the investment of time, in this case, is minimal.

will be able to see the fate of work that is being done with it today.

Vibratory and Tumble Cleaning

Vibratory and tumble cleaning are generally slow ways to clean anything. This is particularly true of the kinds of vibratory cleaning devices that are sold to ammunition reloaders for cleaning and polishing brass shell casings. Similarly, the tumble cleaners sold for amateur rock polishing are limited in size and use. Both are also the kinds of devices that tend to find their ways into automotive cleaning use.

Industrial tumble and vibratory cleaners are expensive and are designed for large volume cleaning jobs. They are designed for continuous or large batch cleaning, jobs that are usually way beyond the scope of non-production uses.

This vibratory cleaner is designed for cleaning shell casings. It is shown here loaded with pulverized walnut shell and liquid polish media. It thoroughly cleans and polishes its contents in a couple of hours. This beats trying to hold small items against a wire brush.

Vibratory cleaners simply vibrate objects in a media of cutting or polishing abrasives. Often, cleaning is started with rough abrasives and moves to progressively finer abrasives, or polishing media. In this process the tub of abrasives and parts is vibrated mechanically to cause friction between the parts and the media, and between the parts themselves. High-end vibratory cleaners have ramping features that parade the parts from the start of the process to its end, at which point they are vibrated out of the tub onto a conveyor (or other means) to be moved to the next grade of abrasives or another process.

Tumbling cleaners contain parts and media in a rotating drum. Cement mixers are often used in low-end applications of this process. As with vibratory cleaning, tumble cleaning may employ many stages, with different abrasives, drum speeds, etc., to affect final cleaning results.

Both vibratory and tumble cleaning are slow compared to other means in terms of the overall time required. On the other hand, vibratory and tumble cleaning devices require little operator input beyond loading and unloading parts and abrasives. In this, they may compare favorably to manually applied abrasive blasting and other approaches with which the operator is one-on-one with each item or surface that is cleaned.

You guessed it: a kid's rock polisher. It also works well on small metal parts, but it's slow. Still, if you have a lot of small parts to clean and are not in any great hurry, this is one way to clean them with very little effort. Larger tumblers are available.

I have found that vibratory and tumbling approaches are particularly useful when many small parts must be cleaned. This is especially true of small items, including fasteners, because they are difficult to hold or fixture for many cleaning processes, such as rotary wire brushing, and because a lot of human time can be saved by cleaning them with vibratory or tumbling batch approaches. With small parts, rock polishers and ammunition vibratory devices can be not only efficient but also extremely effective.

Molten Salt Bath Cleaning

Molten salt bath cleaning is squarely in the province of a heavy-duty industrial cleaning method. Although used mostly in primary metal manufacturing and processing, molten salt bath cleaning is often used by high-volume automotive engine and other component rebuilders to clean crankshafts, cylinder heads, engine blocks, connecting rods, valves, and various other small stamped, forged, and cast parts. Its use is primarily to clean heavy ferrous parts because it employs temperatures that can change the characteristics of some aluminum alloy parts, depending on the alloys involved.

In this process, parts are immersed in molten salts, such as alkaline hydroxides, for periods that are typically less than an hour. Temperatures in the 700 to 800 degrees F range are applied to liquefy the salts and to incinerate any organic contaminants on the parts that are cleaned. The effect of high-temperature salts on dirty automobile parts is to sludge or vaporize any organic substances (paint, oil, grease, etc.) from their surfaces. Sludge can be removed easily from the baths as necessary. This process does not directly remove rust, but it can weaken its structure, which makes its removal later on by other methods much easier.

Molten salt cleaning is mentioned here because the automotive rebuilding and remanufacturing industries find it quite useful. However, given the size, cost, and hazards involved in operating this process, my recommendation is, "Don't try this at home." It can be beneficial to know about some processes, even if you may never use them.

For example, if I was given a choice between a rebuilt engine with parts cleaned by this method or an engine with parts cleaned by other methods, and all other factors were roughly equal, I would likely choose the engine from the molten salt bath. This cleaning method is thorough and tends to anneal and stress relieve parts that are subjected to it, which can be a definite plus.

Hot Galvanizing

While I am on the topic of cleaning by immersion in very hot substances, I should mention hot galvanizing as a combined cleaning and coating process. Several companies provide this service and operate "zinc pots" on a commercial basis.

In this process, chassis and unitized bodies are dipped into molten zinc for varying periods, depending on their complexity and condition. The dipping removes all organic, and some inorganic, material from their surfaces by vaporizing them at temperatures of about 800 degrees F. The results are accomplished by methods very similar to molten salt baths.

The zinc coatings that remain on molten zinc–dipped items protect them from further corrosion, much as galvanizing protected the 2-gallon mop pail that your grandmother used. Another advantage is that zinc is a sacrificial ion coating. This means that if it is scratched or breached in any way, zinc ions migrate into the breach and continue the anti-corrosion protection.

The bragging rights for claiming that your car's chassis or body has been hot dip galvanized must be enormous, because these coatings are very thick and hugely protective against corrosion. Note that hot dip galvanizing deposits a much more substantial coating than do the modern electroplated galvanizing treatments used on the body panels of many new cars.

This process has found favor with some British car restorers. It is touted highly as a way to corrosion-proof the otherwise impossible to reach insides of the box frames used in many collectible British cars. Of course, it also protects their outer surfaces. However, several caveats exist regarding galvanizing as a cleaning and coating measure. It is an expensive service and it is offered in only a few locations. You may have to go great distances to find a good galvanizing facility that accepts a contaminated car body or frame.

Hot dip galvanizing, by its nature, leaves a somewhat rough and sometimes knobby surface that can provide considerable painting challenges. It is also possible that this process may alter surface dimensions. Finally, the high temperatures involved in hot dip galvanizing can warp and distort sheet-metal surfaces, from body panels to frames.

If you choose this approach, be sure that your provider knows what he/she is doing and has had considerable experience with vehicle parts such as the ones that you want treated.

CHOOSING THE BEST CLEANING PROCESSES

This chapter contains a very special feature, which is historic. I will announce the very best cleaning process for all metals, for all purposes, and for anyone who will ever have to clean metal. May I have the envelope, please?

[Drum roll] And the winner is . . .

Sorry, it just isn't that simple. No single process is best for all jobs. It never will be. Too many variables are involved in complex cleaning situations, which is most of them. Different cleaning approaches have advantages, drawbacks, and incompatibilities. For example, using steel wire brushes can be fine for cleaning steel or iron, but can cause irreparable problems on aluminum or plastic. Also, steel and stainless steel brushes tend to polish surfaces. Those surfaces then generally need a sanding operation to guarantee good paint adhesion.

Using steel wool, or even a steel brush, to clean aluminum is a definite no-no. Tiny amounts of steel deposited on aluminum surfaces can cause contamination and subsequent electrolytic corrosion under whatever paint you apply to them. In some cases this may not matter, but in others, it will.

Another example of incompatibility: Cleaning plastic with a stiff hand or motorized steel bristle brush risks scratching it deeply, or melting it. Some processes do not work on some materials.

The problem of using steel tools to clean aluminum has gained considerable attention recently. Ford's first vehicle with a high-volume aluminum alloy body was its 2015

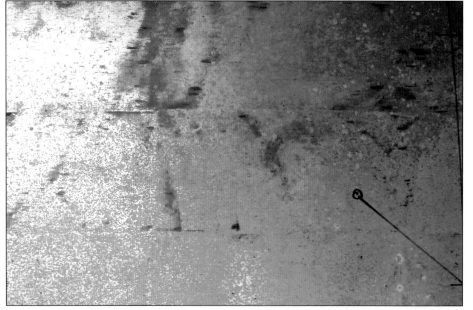

Speaking of complex cleaning situations, recognize this one? It's a deteriorating galvanized steel surface. It combines residues of preservative oil, oxidized zinc coating, and good undamaged surface. Do you remove all of the galvanizing and start from scratch, or try to preserve what is sound? That's a good question with many answers.

Ford F-150 truck. Ford dealers and independent body shops are scrambling to learn the appropriate ways to clean aluminum and to keep it from becoming contaminated after it is cleaned. That is because aluminum must be worked on in isolation from contact with ferrous tools and dust. That dictates tools and environments separate from those used to repair steel-bodied cars and trucks. True, there is a certain, small amount of iron inherent in aluminum, but depositing iron on aluminum surfaces is a different matter.

Grinding dust and tools contaminated with either metal can cause massive corrosion problems with panels and structures made from the other metal. These are problems that fester under primer and paint, until they destroy the work that has been done over this metallic contamination. The solutions to this problem are neither convenient nor inexpensive. Separate tools and equipment are required for each metal, along with separate facilities with separate ventilating systems. This can be done with partitions in the same building, or better, in separate buildings.

The same kinds of problems affect other cleaning processes and other kinds of items that you may have to clean. You shouldn't use the same cleaning approach for aluminum,

Plastic intake manifolds, such as this one, are common in modern engines. Blasting and/or scraping its flanges with a steel scraper can ruin it. Plastic scrapers and chemical gasket removers are in order for this delicate cleaning job.

This cast-iron and aluminum manifold pair presents a simple cleaning job. The flanges on both can be cleaned with a light bead blast. Note that the cast-iron manifold has an expensive porcelain finish that is still in pretty good shape. It should be protected from any blasting application.

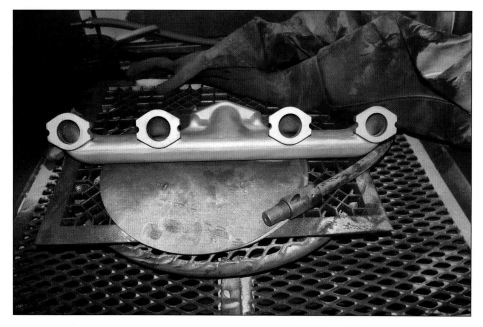

After a light bead blasting, the aluminum manifold in the previous photograph looked like this. It was re-blasted in a dedicated aluminum-only cabinet with media that wasn't contaminated from cleaning steel or iron. It can now be primed with a reactive primer and recoated in its original black color.

steel, or iron, or for plastic flanges, including those on intake manifolds. Each material mandates its own unique cleaning approaches.

I'll continue with the example of the intake manifold. Steel and iron manifolds can be wire brushed with either hand-operated or electrically driven wire brushes with no ill effects and good cleaning results. This is an efficient way to approach cleaning them; but try power wire brushing a plastic manifold and you will destroy it. Aluminum won't fare much better under the assault of a steel wire brush mounted on a 4- or 4½–inch grinder. It may look fine when you are finished brushing it, but may later develop a hard black corrosion that necessitates the milling or sanding of a new surface onto it that is below the electrolytic corrosion that the ferrous contamination caused. What works well in one situation may tempt disaster in another.

Then, there is the issue of what you are trying to remove when you clean something such as a manifold flange. A process that removes rust or

carbon effectively may not work to remove silicone gasket residues from a manifold flange.

Here's an idea. What about taking the manifold that needs its flanges cleaned and bead blasting them in an abrasive blasting cabinet? It might be a bit rough on that plastic manifold, but it should work for a steel, iron, or aluminum manifold. Right?

Well, yes and no. It's probably overkill for the job, and there is the ever-present risk of cross-contaminating the aluminum with

steel blasting debris mixed in with the glass bead. There are simpler ways to clean manifold flanges. And if you decide to clean an intake manifold with glass bead, beware of the fact that one single bead that you may have left behind in the manifold can easily burn and destroy a valve when [not "if"] it gets loose in a valve port and lodges between a valve face and its seat. Glass beads are incredibly rugged, and just one of them on a valve face or seat can hold the valve open minutely until hot exhaust

I love bamboo grilling sticks and toothbrushes for poking into the intricacies of delicate items such as this nameplate. They are cheap, effective, and safe; just the ticket for removing dirt and oxidation from this proud escutcheon. However, trying to clean an engine block with them would be inefficient in the extreme.

gasses streaming through the leak get past the trapped bead and burn the valve, or its seat, or both.

Oh, and if that flange had ever been sealed with a silicone RTV sealant, that substance can contaminate the glass bead in your cabinet and make anything else blasted in it very difficult to paint. The fried oil and grease on that manifold may also contaminate the bead in your cabinet if you don't completely remove them before you blast. So, beading those flanges requires a pre-cleaning, degreasing, and silicone removal step, at the very least.

As you can see from this example, cleaning choices are never simple or completely clear cut. Most often, several interrelated issues underlie them.

Large among these issues is efficiency. If all that you cared about was not harming the surfaces that you clean and doing a really great job cleaning them, you could, I suppose, resort to cleaning them by repeatedly assaulting them with the pointed ends of bamboo fondue sticks and/or using soft toothbrushes on them. This would reduce the chances of inflicting damage to or contamina-

tion on bare metal to a minimum. However, before I wax rhapsodic about the great potential cleaning abilities of fondue sticks and soft toothbrushes, we must admit that this would be one of the slowest methods of cleaning automobile parts and surfaces that the human mind has ever conceived or considered. Scratch those two.

At the other extreme are approaches such as 36-grit sanding discs (boulder edition) and silica carbide blasting media delivered at high pressure. If these media are used without great caution they can overheat, stretch, and cut through metal parts in very short order. Yes, they are fast, but much too fast and brutal for most automotive cleaning

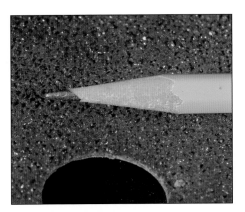

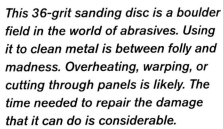

This 36-grit sanding disc is a boulder field in the world of abrasives. Using it to clean metal is between folly and madness. Overheating, warping, or cutting through panels is likely. The time needed to repair the damage that it can do is considerable.

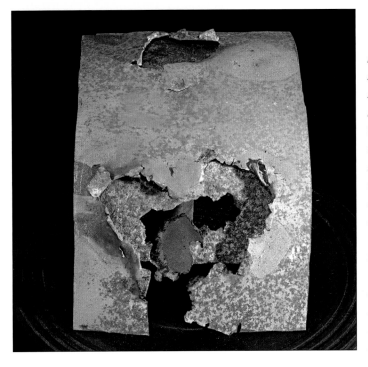

Not a pretty sight! This fender section has been blasted through the 18-gauge outer metal and, in some places, the reinforcing layer under it. Damage such as this can occur fairly quickly with aggressive abrasives shot at high pressures. Repairing it is a long, slow job.

Paint removers of various types have been around for decades. Some work faster than others. All of them are messy to use and none can completely avoid the problem of residues trapped in part and panel details. Trapped residue emerges eventually to destroy the paint job.

jobs, as some folks have found out to their great dismay. What you need is a balance. You need to balance the need for efficiency and speed with the imperative to protect parts from collateral cleaning damage.

In general, the safest and most available process is the one that you should use. I say available because the best process is often unavailable. Hot dip galvanizing and molten salt baths may be ideal for some jobs, but are very difficult to find and likely very expensive for just a few items, if you can even find them. The choice between, say, a disc sander for stripping a car or one of several abrasive blasting processes is more a matter of what is available to you and what you are comfortable using.

Let's say that you have neither a disc sander nor access to abrasive blasting equipment. What remains most available is chemical paint strippers and hand sanding. Those processes may not be ideal, but they are what you have. So you may be limited to making a choice between these two approaches.

Generally, chemical processes are available at some level. Dip tanks are harder to access than paint remover, which is readily available. All chemical processes remove paint, but only high-end chemical processes remove rust. That is worth considering before you go that route. Chemical processes, and for that matter all wet processes, tend to be messy and pose the hazard of leaving chemical residues behind in the nooks and crannies of parts and panels. That can come back and cause paint failure months or years after they are used.

Surface abrasion processes, including various sanding approaches, are either comparatively slow (DA and jitterbug sanding) or require great skill to avoid damage (disc sanding). However, while the skill level for sanding equipment may be high, the cost of the equipment is usually at the low end of cleaning equipment.

The Great Bare Metal Debate

When was the last time that you heard someone say something like this when bragging about a refinishing or restoration job: "Of course, we took her to bare metal. That's the only right way to do the job." You probably nodded in assent. The bare metal obsession used to impress me, mostly because I was aware of the great effort that it takes to completely strip a car of all paint and rust; and most often, it's required.

However, as time went on I began to notice that some cars that were originally painted in enamels still looked pretty good after 30 or 40 years of service, at least where they hadn't been hit or scraped. I even noticed panels on some cars in junkyards that still looked good after years of exposure to the elements in their outdoor life. Often, the only problem with their paint was that surface oxidation had dulled and/or chalked it. You could easily sand or compound many of these original finishes to expose the serviceable paint under that surface oxidation, long before you got to bare metal. And when you did get there, usually there was no sign that your excavation to bare metal had taken you through rust.

Over the years I experimented with preserving sound basecoats by sanding into them until I came to sound paint. Occasionally, I would have to take a rusted spot to bare metal and then treat it with a metal conditioner before I built its surface back up to the level of the surrounding paint. I never had a paint failure in any panel that I had treated that way. My approach of preserving sound undercoats saved time and money, and it worked well. I just

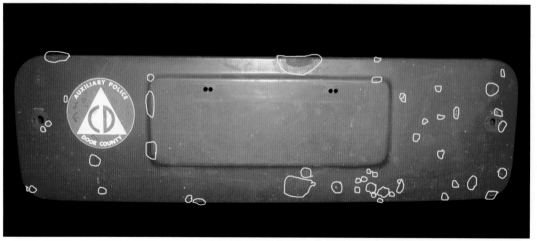

This sports car tire compartment cover would usually be completely refinished, given its number of paint defects. However, the car's owner chose to build a new finish on the original finish to preserve the original Civil Defense decal. He didn't want to lose it. The major defects are circled.

didn't have the bragging rights of having taken a car to bare metal.

Here is what I am *not* saying. If you have a body or a panel that is suffering from rust coming through paint, rust under paint, crumbling paint, and the like, no attempt to preserve it will succeed, because you do not have the foundation over which to build a sound finish. In these cases you have to remove all paint, primer, and rust and start building your new finish up from bare metal. But if you can sand an old finish to basically sound undercoats, including primer, undercoats with only a few, minor exceptions to sound paint, it *may* be a good idea to repair the damaged areas and preserve those original undercoats as a foundation on which to build up new topcoats.

If this sounds radical, that is probably because it is very conservative. It conserves what is sound and good in a painting situation, and it can save time and money. However, it requires good judgment and skill, because you have to know when and how to evaluate paint to make the decision to preserve it. You also need considerable skill to make any needed repairs to the coats that you are saving, and you have to condition them properly before you can build a finish over them.

Although the bulk of this book is devoted to how to clean metal, it is still important to know when it might be best not to clean metal, or, at least, when to consider not "going all the way," that is, cleaning metal selectively. It is definitely *not* my intention to provide a rationale for painting over any unsound or ratty old finish to create a basis for a new finish. Despite the enormous capabilities of modern sealers and barrier coats, these shields have their limits.

In making a decision not to clean to bare metal, you might want to consider this. When cars were originally painted their finishes were applied under what were then ideal conditions. The metal on which finishes were built was absolutely as clean as it could be. It had been degreased, pickled or phosphated, and coated as quickly as practicable with primer and waterproof topcoats. Later, by the 1970s, as unitized construction broadly replaced body-on-frame approaches, it became common to e-coat bodies after pickling them. This involved using cathodic attraction to literally pull and bond the first coating into their surfaces

Painting was performed under near-ideal conditions. First there was the paint. It was formulated to specifications that aftermarket paints could not match. It was, and remains, different from the paints that are available in the aftermarket. Factory enamels were reflow paints.

Sometimes, you need to go to bare metal in a few very small spots in an otherwise sound finish. The tip of the small pad on a vibratory sander (left) or one of the fiberglass stick sanders (left to right in descending diameters) might be the perfect tool for this job.

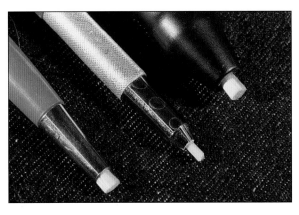

The tiny fiberglass scratch brush in the center is ideal for removing rust and paint from small areas. The larger scratch pens beside it work well with larger spots. Always wear breathing and eye protection when using these tools. They release small fiberglass fragments that can be dangerous.

After paint application, bodies were baked for 30 minutes or more at 160 to 180 degrees F to soften and reflow them. This bonded the paints to their undercoats and gave them additional flatness and luster. All of these materials and processes were almost perfectly consistent, and so were their results.

Then there was the finishing environment. Temperature and humidity were perfectly controlled. The air in paint rooms and in paint lines was absolutely clean, and painting equipment was maintained perfectly. As good as some modern body shops are, they cannot come close to matching the conditions of the initial application of finishes to vehicles.

The point is, if you have a vehicle or panel that was originally painted under the conditions that I just described, you should realize that you probably can never replicate the favorable conditions that were present when it was initially painted. Some very advanced restoration facilities can come close, particularly the ones that restore large volumes of cars, but I doubt if they can ever quite reach the standards of original factory paint.

If you have a vehicle with paint that is still structurally sound, showing only some surface defects and deterioration, it may make great sense to preserve that foundation and build a new finish over it. First, consider whether the surface qualifies: It must have very few and very small areas of defect that require repair before the overcoat. Be careful to use appropriate barrier coatings and sealers, which may be required to prevent ugly defects such as sand scratch swelling. Finally, you have to make sure that you do not build up a coating that's too thick, because if you do, it may craze and/or crack from temperature changes.

With all of that said, your best choice sometimes is to repair and overcoat a factory finish. Look at it this way: Considering the advantages that the factory had when it painted a car, if an original finish has survived intact for decades with little or no evidence of structural defect, it is a good candidate for surviving a lot longer. Often, properly repairing a few bad spots and sealing the finish may be the best approach. It's difficult to argue with long-term, proven adhesion.

After sanding out a small rust spot, this scratch pen was used to feather sand the surrounding paint. This was followed with light finger sanding with 320-grit paper before primer was applied to the area. A second sanding further feathered the edge and created a good profile for primer adhesion.

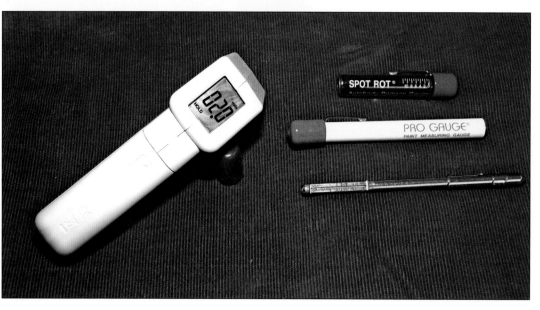

To salvage an old finish as the base for a new one, you must know the old finish's thickness. The digital gauge on the left reads coating mil thickness with great accuracy. The magnetic gauges on the right read thickness fairly accurately. The one on top can read filler thickness.

Selective Stripping and Masking Issues

Depending on how you decide "The Great Bare Metal Debate," you need to either completely strip a car or panel to bare metal or try to preserve the sound layers of paint that you find as the basis for building a new finish. If you adopt the latter approach, removing the unsound topcoats and preserving the basecoats, you need to find processes that allow you to make this selection. Disc sanding and many abrasive media blasting approaches are far too fast to allow selective removal of layers of paint.

Sanding with a DA sander is slow, but may allow you to sand coats selectively, particularly if they are refinish coats over original paint. Because topcoats and primer coats are usually

The large particle, high-quality soda in this bag is ideal for selectively removing paint layers from bodies. You can set blast pressure and maintain target angles and distances to make this easy. Another plus for this stripping method is that you don't have to mask glass and trim.

different colors, it is often possible to use a slow removal process, such as DA sanding, with relatively fine abrasive grits to selectively remove topcoats. Unfortunately, while this approach offers good safety for preserving undercoats, it can be slow work.

Most abrasive blasting approaches are too fast to be used selectively and tend to abrade, stretch, and destroy the very adhesion layers that you are trying to preserve. Sharp media particles such as aluminum oxide and quartz sand tend to cut into paint uncontrollably, while peening media such as glass beads stretch paint and destroy its adhesion to substrates.

Two media groups work particularly well for slow and selective coating removal: plastic media blasting (PMB) and soda blasting. Both can be used to remove paint coatings aggressively and fairly quickly, but they can also be tuned down (pressure, particle size, and blast gun angle and distance-from-target) to remove coatings slowly and selectively.

Conclusions and Other Factors

Several factors must be considered to make good choices of metal cleaning methods. With some cleaning processes it is easy to protect areas that you do not want to subject to your cleaning actions. Manual and mechanical sanding processes tend to fit into this category. With these methods, you have the simple

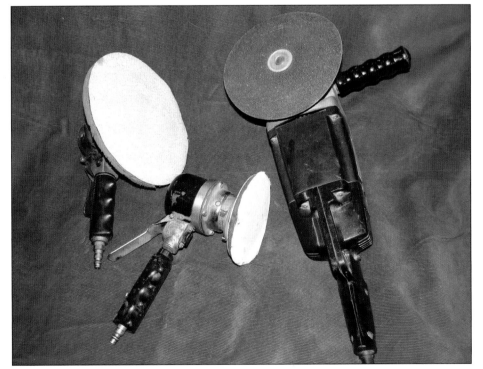

The DA sanders on the left, an 8-inch and a 5-inch, work slowly and gently. They are ideal for selectively removing layers of old paint but are too slow for general stripping. The disc sander on the right works too quickly for selective stripping but is great for uncovering bare metal.

option of avoiding the areas that you want to protect.

With chemical methods it is sometimes possible to protect specific areas from cleaning agents, but it is difficult and cumbersome to do so. If spot and/or area protection is important, chemical cleaning is probably not your best choice.

Abrasive blast cleaning allows for protecting areas from blast. This is done with soft plugs and resilient tapes, or even paints. Blast media tends to bounce off soft, resilient surfaces. Blasted signs and marker stones are often lettered by using resilient tape letters and blasting around them, or soft stencils for the opposite effect. The same method can be used to protect areas on blasted objects, such as threaded holes. The need to protect some areas may enter into your determination of the best cleaning process, or variation of that process, for a specific job.

A related issue is cleaning damage. Some metal cleaning propositions dictate what can and cannot be done. For example, for all practical purposes, wire wheels are too intricate to clean with mechanical sanding processes. They should be cleaned chemically or with abrasive blasting approaches. Because they are structural, how they are cleaned becomes a safety consideration. For example, if wire wheels are plated, an obvious approach to cleaning them is to use reverse plating.

But if this approach is chosen, and the wheels have welded spokes, hydrogen embrittlement is a serious and very dangerous possibility with reverse plating, unless specific measures are taken to overcome hydrogen embrittlement of their welds. This kind of consideration is critical in choosing appropriate cleaning processes. The potential for damage is always there if you use an inappropriate process.

Other kinds of cleaning damage are more common: warping sheet metal with blast media and leaving residues with wet processes, such as slurry blasting and immersion cleaning, etc. No simple set of rules exists for avoiding cleaning damage. The best protection is to know and understand the hazards associated with each cleaning process and equipment type that you employ. Research is the key to exercising this kind of vigilance. Know the potential downsides of all processes, equipment, and materials that you are using to clean metal.

I have alluded to efficiency in cleaning several times. Different processes create different sweet spots in terms of efficiencies. Picking the paint out of the rough areas of a bronze nameplate casting may be a good approach to cleaning it. But it would be ludicrous to use that method to clean the outside of a cylinder block casting, unless the casting is for a model airplane engine. Within the limits of economic factors and availability, try to choose the best process for the scale of what you are attempting to clean.

It is easy to continue to use an inefficient process, just because you started with it. Avoid this temptation. As you work with a cleaning process, constantly evaluate its relevance to what you are trying to accomplish. If it took you a day to DA sand a door, you might want to switch to a faster alternative before you find that you have spent ten days stripping an auto body.

This is not to say that the fastest process is the best one. But a process that is quick, that is accessible to you, and that produces a high-quality result is preferable to one that much more slowly produces the same result. Similar logic suggests that if a job is small, it is less critical to maximize the speed and/or efficiency with which it is accomplished. What might seem an unacceptably inefficient approach to stripping an entire car could be fine for stripping a glove box door or a hinged fuel door.

A similar consideration involves equipment, supplies, and purchased services. A $6,000 or $7,000 steam cleaner is a wonder to behold. You can strip the grease, grime, and tar off a chassis more quickly than by any other method that occurs to me. But how many chassis will you strip in a year? How many other jobs will such a rig reasonably accomplish for you? If it takes a day, or a day and a half, to manually strip a frame with solvent, scrapers, sanders, or blasters, it is probably a good tradeoff versus spending several thousand dollars for equipment that you will rarely use.

By the same logic, if you are a serial car restorer or incorrigible customizer, it probably makes sense to own a good blast cabinet for dealing with the medium-size parts that you will likely need to clean. In these propositions, your own labor is always the floating factor. It is best not to undervalue it in favor of making massive and marginal equipment purchases, or to overvalue it by spending hours doing what good and affordable equipment can do for you with much greater efficiency.

There, I've probably managed to offend the relevant parties at both ends of my proposition, the sellers of expensive equipment and the spouses of the people who long for it.

FRANK WEINERT, MASTER BLASTER AND MAN ABOUT CARS

I once asked Bob Lorkowski, the genial and highly knowledgeable proprietor of the fabulous L'Cars restoration shops in Cameron and Bruce, Wisconsin, as well as the Classic Auto Collision Center in Bruce how he stripped the cars that he restores. Please understand that L'Cars restores some of the most fabulous and expensive cars on the planet, as well as many other interesting vehicles. Further know that it does this work to standards that are shatteringly high in anyone's judgment. L'Cars routinely tackles some of the most difficult restorations imaginable.

Bob's answer to my question surprised me. He said, "We sandblast them. How would *you* strip vehicles for restoration?" My response probably didn't surprise him.

"But, but, but, aren't you afraid that you'll stretch and warp panels, and maybe cut through fragile ones?"

"No," he said, "We have a way to avoid those problems."

Incredulously, I asked, "Wanna share it?"

"Sure," he said. "I never let anyone blast a panel or car unless he has several years of experience restoring sheet metal."

The incredible wisdom of that statement still astounds me. How better to guard against blasting damage than to employ blast operators who are fully aware of the great harm that this process can do to thin metal when

Frank Weinert is a master of abrasive blasting. He is seen here starting to soda blast a door from a mid-century GM truck that he is restoring. You are looking at him through the windshield opening of the cab of that truck, which he has already finished soda blasting.

This is what the cab of the truck looked like after Frank had blasted selected areas of it where he had made repairs to the metal. What you see here indicates the general condition of the truck body as he received it, with some sound metal and some rusted metal.

This hood, not part of the GM truck, was soda and sand blasted, but had become contaminated before it could be protected. Here, Frank is cleaning and neutralizing its metal with a cleaning and preservative spray to stabilize it for later sandblasting. He is using PPG DX330 for this purpose.

it is used without fine judgment? It makes perfect sense. You might call it the basis of a great "incentive plan."

Recently, I had occasion to spend some time with Bob's abrasive blaster, Frank Weinert, and to learn some of his approaches to his craft. At the outset, please note that Frank is expert at all aspects of vehicle restoration. In his shop he welds, fabricates, bumps metal, fills, refinishes, and the rest of the full range of body restoration endeavors. He also works on engines and drivelines, and operates an impressive machine shop. He is one of the few people I've met who really can "do it all." Well, maybe, almost all. Some tasks, such as plating and upholstery, may be beyond his capabilities.

The day that I visited Frank he was blast cleaning the cab and doors for a mid–20th century GM truck. He applied his standard approach to this job. I'll go over it in detail later, but in broad outline his approach to sheetmetal cleaning has five basic elements:

Step 1. Pre-clean the body or parts, as necessary, to remove grease and grime, if any.

Step 2. Blast the parts or body with bicarbonate of soda to remove paint and loose rust.

Step 3. Blast paint residues and deep rust out of any areas where the soda blasting did not completely remove them with quartz sand, particularly in high-crown areas. Use extreme caution in low-crown areas to avoid any warping or distortion of metal there with the quartz sandblasting.

Step 4. Use a small mechanical mesh disc to remove any remaining deep, pitted rust.

Step 5. Protect cleaned metal from new corrosion by applying a

Soda blasting the flat back panel of the cab is a very safe way to remove the paint and loose rust from it. Note Frank's close blasting distance and his very perpendicular blast angle. There isn't much rust under the paint in this area because the paint here is pretty sound.

After Frank soda blasted the GM cab, he sandblasted it. Note that he is using a much greater gun-to-target distance than in soda blasting, and a more acute blast angle. A lot of the rust that the soda blasting couldn't remove is now being sandblasted off the metal.

After sand and soda blasting sheet metal, Frank uses a drill-motor-driven 3-inch 3M Scotch-Brite Roloc disc to remove remaining rust that has resisted his blasting processes. Almost any blasting regimen that doesn't warp sheet metal requires some degree of mechanical follow-up after blasting is completed.

self-etching primer as soon as is practical after completing the abrasive blasting steps.

These steps will be discussed in detail as we follow that GM truck cab and doors through Frank's process.

Frank's Soda-Blasting Process

The first thing that Frank does is to remove all loose dirt and grime from the item or body that he is stripping (Step 1). The truck cab that we follow in this chapter had not required any pre-cleaning measures. Some areas, where metal repairs were needed, had already been blasted and the repairs made before I started to photograph Frank's stripping process. Most of the stripping work remained to be done.

Pre-cleaning a raw body, such as this one, can be accomplished in many ways, depending on its underlying condition and on the kind and amount of soil that has to be removed. Pressure washing with detergent, steam cleaning, and solvent spraying or brushing are the standard approaches to this job.

Frank's next step is to soda blast all body surfaces (Step 2). In the case of this cab, soda blasting removed most paint and all loose surface rust. It did not remove all of the rust because soda is not an aggressive enough media to cut through and remove deep, pitted rust or strongly adhered surface rust. That stubborn surface contamination will be removed during sandblasting (Step 3).

So, you might ask, "Why not just sandblast the cab and doors in the first place, and skip the soda blasting altogether, reducing two operations to one?" After all, sandblasting more easily and quickly removes anything

that soda will. The reason for Frank's two-stage approach is that soda blasting takes care of about 90 percent of the contaminants that you need to remove from the truck cab and doors' metal surfaces, with absolutely no damage to the metal. Although that

percentage varies somewhat with the condition of what you are stripping, soda blasting is almost always a useful first step. Most of the surface is clean after soda blasting. The important point is that 90 percent of the cleaning was accomplished

Here is the GM cab in Frank's shop, ready for complete soda and sandblasting. Only the areas where metal repairs were made have already been blasted. All of the metal that remains is now basically sound, but contaminated with paint and rust in varying degrees.

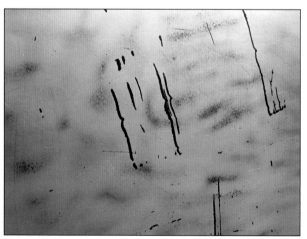

The truck's soda-blasted rear panel surface looked like this. Some traces of primer and paint and some deep, pitted vertical rust streaks are visible. It's always interesting to speculate what caused these rust streaks. My best guess is deep scratches or a chemical splash that compromised the paint.

with absolutely no danger or damage to the metal. And, for a bonus, soda blasting revealed exactly where more severe measures would have to be taken.

Unlike the sandblasting that will follow soda blasting in this job, soda blasting does not stretch, distort, or warp sheet metal. Also unlike sandblasting, soda blasting requires no special skill to avoid those pitfalls. Although soda blasting is aggressive enough to remove most surface contaminants, it is not strong enough to do any physical damage to metal, even delicate metal.

"But," you might well ask, "why not just use soda and avoid sandblasting altogether?" That is another fair question. The answer is that the residues that you see on this truck cab (some surface rust, some pitted rust, and even a few spots of stubborn primer and paint) did not yield to soda blasting in a reasonable amount of time. The leading virtue of soda blasting is that it is mild and easy on metal, but its corresponding drawback is that there are some well-adhered contaminants that it just cannot successfully attack. Soda blasting also does not leave steel with a surface profile (anchor pattern or tooth) that mechanically bonds primer. Sandblasting adds those features to surfaces. That's it in a nutshell.

Soda blasting had another advantage in this two-stage blasting process. It took Frank down to the areas that will need sandblasting without endangering the sheet metal. That allows him to see what specific spots and areas need additional attention, without subjecting the panels to possible damage just to reveal those spots and areas. That is a huge advantage in the battle to clean metal without damaging it. It greatly reduces the amount of potentially damaging sandblasting because the worst areas can be found without using the more aggressive sandblasting process to find them.

Soda Blasting Step by Step

The photographs in this section detail Frank's approach to soda blasting the GM truck cab. Please notice several items. Frank is wearing eye, lung, ear, and body protection that is adequate for the job. Some people would argue for more protection, particularly lung protection in the form of an outside air breathing supply, but since this is outdoor blasting on an occasional basis, his lung protection is probably sufficient.

Frank uses varied approaches on the different areas that he is blasting. The only constants are that he is blasting with 90-psi air pressure through a half-inch nozzle and using relatively large-particle bicarbonate of soda-blasting media. His angle to target, distance to target, and pass speed vary according to the needs of the situation.

The distance and angle variables are evident in the photographs. Where paint removal is the main concern, he tends to use a fairly direct angle and a short distance to

1 *This truck cab looks big, compared to Frank's small blast pattern. Still, in less than 2 hours he removed most of the paint and loose rust from its outside panels and inside surfaces with soda blasting. Later he will blast the cab with quartz sand.*

2 Note the fairly straight-on angle that Frank is using to attack mixed paint and rust. Years of experience have taught him that this is the best approach to the area that he is cleaning with soda.

3 As blasting media go, soda is on the soft, non-aggressive end of the scale. However, it has enough cutting power to remove fairly sound paint and adhered surface rust from this old cab's sheet metal.

4 Frank doesn't try to take the cab's surface to absolutely clean metal with soda blasting. That would be inefficient. Part of what he accomplishes with soda is to reveal areas where he must later concentrate his quartz sandblasting to achieve clean metal.

5 Note that Frank's soda attack is almost always on the edge between cleaned and unblasted metal. This is where the soda blast fatigues and deteriorates paint and rust most quickly and efficiently.

6 Attempting to remove the combined paint and rust from a large, flat panel, such as the one on the back of this cab, with sandblasting requires extreme care to avoid warping. Soda does most of this removal job safely. Later, carefully applied sand media finishes the job.

7 Blasting is athletic work. You have to get your blast nozzle in the best position for what you are doing and your eyes in a position that allows you to see what you are doing.

8 *This might look like tedious work, given the small removal patch of each blast pass. In fact, Frank is moving so quickly that it requires his full attention to make efficient use of the blast.*

9 *Frank concentrates his blast on the small rust area that is still visible just under and to the left of his blast. He does this with soda to avoid distorting the metal. The sand media that finishes this job requires a much less concentrated approach than the soda.*

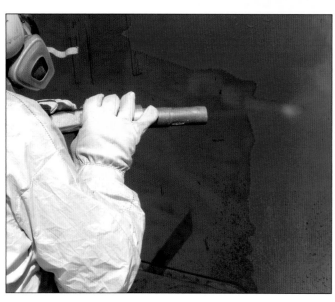

10 *In this relatively rust-free area Frank has adopted a narrower blast angle and is moving faster than he was before. He is also working closer to the surface. You can see the effects of his modified angle on the metal.*

target. Although the width of his blast removal area for paint is fairly narrow, he is moving his blast nozzle at considerable speed.

The day that I visited Frank, his soda-blast work on the cab and doors took a bit more than an hour and consumed somewhere between 150 and 200 pounds of soda.

In some areas, his soda blast left the metal almost free of rust. This was particularly true in the massive rear panel of the cab. This is the area where the paint was soundest, where it took the most time to remove it with soda. Obviously, its exposure to ultraviolet light and pooled moisture was less than, say, the roof. Because of this panel's lack of crown (its flatness), it is the area that would be easiest to warp and distort with the sand media blasting that will follow the soda-blasting operation (Step 3).

The cab's vertical back panel is where Frank used the shortest gun-to-target distances, thus employing the smallest blast pattern. That was possible because it is also where the metal benefited from the best protection from rust and was therefore the least rusted. Usually, rust is more difficult to remove than old paint.

The rear corners of the cab were another story. Here, the paint was badly deteriorated and came off easily under soda blasting. However, this is also where the cab suffered the most extensive rust damage and where the soda blast was least effective. The last photos in this section makes this point graphically.

The good news is that high-crown areas, such as the cab corners, are best able to withstand the assault of sandblasting without warping or distorting.

11 The bottom corners of the cab show more rust damage than the rest of it. This is due to gravel impacts. Note that Frank is banding a blast area before he attacks it. This is a standard approach.

12 In this photograph, you get some idea of the amount of soda that is being directed at the cab. It amounts to a bit under one pound per minute.

13 The upper corners of the cab also show considerable surface rusting, due to deterioration of the paint in the upper cab from exposure to the sun. This is different from the gravel damage–induced rust on the lower cab corners.

14 Frank uses a very close nozzle distance and direct angle to reduce a stubborn rust spot as much as possible with soda.

15 As he reaches less rusted metal, Frank pulls his nozzle away from the panel. Good blasting requires constant attention to changing conditions and making adjustments to account for them.

16 Frank finishes soda blasting the cab's rear panel. Notice that some paint and a lot of rust remain on the metal. Sandblasting removes it. The soda blasting has made it much easier to see where sandblasting is needed.

17 The rounded metal in the bend areas from the back to the side panels can withstand more blasting than the flat metal around it without warping or distorting. The top and bottom corners are even tougher. Frank limits his soda blasting in these areas but will sandblast them aggressively.

18 Frank soda blasts a replacement sill that he formed and welded into the body where the original sill had rusted out. Soda and sand-blasting this sill gives it the same surface as the rest of the cab's metal when it is painted.

19 Frank ends his soda-blasting job by revisiting one of the worst areas of the cab. A combination of strongly adhered paint and deep rust limit what soda can accomplish here. Carefully applied sandblasting is the only way to ready this area for paint.

Corrosion that remained there after soda blasting was much less problematic than was corrosion on the flat back panel of the cab, where intensive sandblasting could do considerable warping damage to the metal. Even with soda, Frank is keeping his nozzle a close but respectful distance from the metal in the large, flat back panel of the cab.

The upper sides and corners of the roof, as with the lower corners of the cab, are deeply rusted but also high-crown metal. In these areas, too, Frank unleashes the full fury of his soda blast on the metal with little fear of damaging it. He knows from experience that soda never completely removes the rust in these areas and that sandblasting is required to accomplish this, or at least to accomplish most of it.

In the repaired areas where Frank applied sandblasting to surfaces that had already been soda blasted, you can see some of the welds used in the repairs. Here, the soda blast is being used to remove superficial rust and contamination that may have attacked these areas after they were repaired.

Frank is starting to sandblast the fairly low-crown roof of the GM truck cab. He is teasing the metal with his blast, using a gun distance and angle that cannot warp metal. Being tentative when you begin to sandblast a new area can save a lot of grief later.

Frank's Sandblasting Process

The next process is to blast the cab and doors with sand media, in this case quartz sand (Frank's Step 3). This completes the main phase of the surface cleaning job, leaving only small amounts of stubborn contamination for removal by mechanical means (Frank's Step 4).

The key to Frank's success in this critical phase of his cleaning process, blasting with the aggressive quartz sand media, is exercising consistently good judgment based on keen observation and extensive experience. Anyone can point a blast nozzle at a part or panel and blast it clean, and then to oblivion. The real challenge is to sandblast vehicle body metal without causing damage to it.

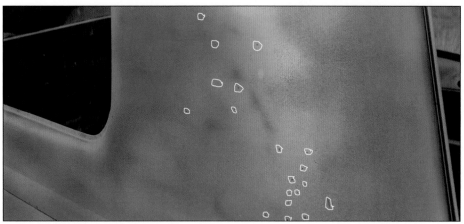

This area cleaned up well with soda blasting; some deep surface pits are visible, mostly in the photo's lower right. There is enough crown there to retard warping by the blast that removes those surface pits. The few deeper pits in this area require mechanical removal.

The damage in question is either warping or cutting through the part or panel. Cutting through is extreme, and rarely occurs with sound metal, unless the person doing the blasting goes completely bananas. More often, it occurs when paint, filler, surface rust, or combinations of those camouflages hide unsound metal. Suddenly, you'll hear a blast operator say

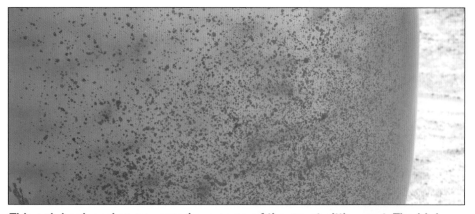

This cab back and corner area have some of the worst pitting rust. The high-crown corner takes a lot more blast energy than the lower-crown back before it starts to warp. The rust here almost certainly came from gravel chips in the paint.

These 100-pound bags of industrial quartz sand are difficult to handle and transport without good equipment. Frank's end loader is just the ticket for this job. Frank doesn't have a lot of fancy equipment for his sandblasting operation, just the right equipment for the job.

With the bags positioned over Frank's blast pot, a small knife slash in each bag begins the unloading process. It takes around a minute, each, to load two bags (200 pounds) into the blast pot. That amount of sand goes a long way toward sandblasting the truck's cab and doors.

Smoothing the sand into his pressure pot, Frank has a chance to look at it and make sure that it is clean and dry. Any moisture or large contamination in the sand or pressurized blast air in his system can waste time and cause frustrating clogging in the sandblast output.

something like, "Oh, @#$%!," and if he or she is a sensitive soul, will burst into tears. More stoic individuals usually just continue blasting while muttering expletives.

Distortion and warping are the more usual damage created in blasting. The mechanism that causes these disasters is often stated erroneously as the heat generated by blasting media hitting their targets. This is the same kind of heat that hand or disc sanding produces: heat from friction. And while heat from an over enthusiastically applied sanding disc can cause local overheating that results in warping and bulging metal, this is not the cause of warping and bulging from abrasive blasting. For one thing, the blast media arrives at-target accompanied by the large volume of cooling air that is propelling it. Some abrasives may cause target metal to give off sparks, which is a sure indication that local heating is occurring. However, the air in the blast quickly dissipates the heat in the blast. A few degrees of surface temperature rise (either Fahrenheit or Celsius) does not warp or distort sheet metal.

A credible explanation for blast-induced warping and distortion must lie elsewhere. Fortunately, it is fairly simple to discover and to comprehend.

When you hit one side of a piece of sheet metal thousands or tens of thousands of times with small projectiles, you'd think that it would be like hitting the metal with something such as a ball peen hammer, but it's not. The blast projectiles aren't big enough and are not hitting the metal hard enough to deform it visibly; they don't put a dent in it. Instead, they are pounding it flatter. On a microscopic level, they are transferring the energy from their impacts against the metal in ways

that compact its surface. This causes the material on the surface to compress and become thinner. It also puts that surface under compressive stress, which makes it tougher. With the right peening media, this process can be employed advantageously to toughen metal. However, with cutting media, such as that used for sandblast stripping, the metal is made thinner and slightly tougher.

As the metal becomes more compressed and thinner on one side, it has to go somewhere. That somewhere is into the metal's lateral dimensions: width and height. The surface becomes longer and wider on the side that is being blasted. However, the rest of the metal under that compressed surface isn't stretched and its lateral dimensions remain unchanged. As they ask in the mystery novels, "Then what happens?"

Inevitably, the metal bulges or warps toward the blast because it has to go somewhere to accommodate the new, increased lateral dimensions on its blast side. It is also restrained by the uncompressed and unexpanded metal around the blasted area, so it has nowhere to go but into a warp or bulge that allows the expanded side and the unexpanded side of the panel to live together.

This is similar to what happens when you heat a thermocouple, a thin metal strip made from two different metals firmly adhered to each other but with different coefficients of expansion. As you heat or cool a thermocouple, one side expands or contracts more than the other. The result is that it curves in a predictable way to accommodate the dimensional changes that occur in its two attached sides.

I have gone into detail on this point for two reasons. It is widely

misunderstood and incorrectly stated as "It's the heat that warps metal in blasting." I once heard the president of a major company that manufactures and sells blast equipment state this incorrect notion as an explanation of absolute fact.

My second reason for stating the correct basis of the blast warping sequence as a major and important fact is that if you understand the mechanism that causes abrasive blast warping, and the distortion that results in making panels bulge and look wavy, then you will be able to understand how to avoid these problems.

One useful way to look at this is to think of abrasive blasting as putting mechanical energy into the metal that you are blasting. If you put too much energy into one place, you create the problems of distortion and warping. Any, all, or any combination of blast variables has the potential for creating distortion in sheet metal. Specifically, using a blast pressure that is too high, blast particles that are too large, a nozzle-to-target distance that is too close, a blast angle that is too perpendicular, or a pass speed that is too slow can cause distortion.

If you think of each of these variables as raising or lowering the energy input into a part or panel, then you can work out combinations of them that do not exceed what is safe for that part or panel. To master this concept and practice requires a lot of observation and experience. (It's best to gain the experience part of this proposition by working with scrap parts and panels and saving important and treasured items for when you already have the necessary blasting experience and won't harm them.)

Sandblasting Step by Step

The photographs in this section illustrate how Frank Weinert sandblasted the GM truck cab and doors with quartz sand. Several things are notable. If you compare the photos of his quartz sandblasting with those of his soda blasting, you immediately notice that the gun's distances-to-target are usually much greater with the sand media than when he is blasting with soda media. In addition, his angle of attack to what he is blasting is much less perpendicular (with sand versus soda). Said another way, he is more accurate with sandblasting.

This is to minimize the risks of warping or otherwise distorting the sheet-metal panels that Frank is blasting. The risk of causing this kind of damage is much greater with a hard media, such as sand, than it is with the much less aggressive soda media.

Although you can see the gun-to-target angle and distance in these photographs, you cannot see Frank's pass speed. It tended to be slower than in soda blasting but at much greater distance from the panels. It is this combination of gun distance, pass speed, and angle that Frank manipulates to avoid damaging the panels that he is sandblasting.

It is particularly important to note the precautions that Frank takes to avoid damaging the truck's panels when he is dealing with low-crown, or relatively flat areas of metal. Higher-crown areas, such as the lower cab corners and corner verticals, are less susceptible to blasting distortion. These high-crown areas are regions of metal that fall away from a point in all directions, although not necessarily in equal amounts. These areas were toughened by work hardening when they were stamped. The more

1 *Soda blasting has removed a lot of rust and paint from the truck cab. The most stubborn stains remain as Frank begins blasting the truck's left door with sand. Soon he will move the door to the ground to get better control of his blasting variables.*

2 *Frank uses the same nozzle size and air pressure with sand media that he used with soda. Sand cuts much faster and can warp the door metal. Note Frank's greatly increased nozzle-to-panel distance and gun angle with the sand media. His dwell time is actually longer.*

3 The roof and upper sides of the cab were more rusted than most of its other areas and were not as thoroughly cleaned by soda blasting. They require more intensive sand blasting than the rest of the cab.

4 In addition to Frank's greater gun-to-target distance with sand media than with soda, he is also employing a slower pass speed. That is necessary to achieve the surface cleaning that he needs with the increased distance. It also gives him better control over any warping or cut-through hazards.

5 One great advantage of blasting outside in open country on a nice day is good light and great accessibility. True, weather can be a problem, but on a nice day outside blasting has many advantages over a blast booth, particularly when media recovery is not an issue.

6 Even though most of the cabin's interior metal surfaces will never be seen after this restoration is completed, Frank cleans them meticulously.

7 Frank is approaching an extremely critical area as he begins to blast the cab roof. The high-crown area, that is, the compound curve transition area from the roof's sides, is tough and resists warping and distortion. The relatively flat top of the roof does not.

8 Note that Frank employs an extremely sharp angle of attack and a very long distance to target as he moves from the high-crown area of the roof into its flatter area.

deformed metal is in the stamping process, the more work hardened it becomes. Because this makes the metal tougher, it better resists the high-energy blasting that occurs with sand media.

Another factor that tends to preserve high-crown panel areas under the assault of sandblasting is that any distortion that does occur in them is less noticeable and less of a problem; the distortion tends to flow into uniform curvature without bulging the panel in ways that are noticeable or look wavy. A little distortion in a low-crown panel quickly becomes visible and, perhaps worse, is difficult to correct.

When Frank blasted the very flat and badly rusted roof panel, he maintained large gun-to-target distances and relatively acute angles of attack. This helped to make up for his slow pass speed.

The surfaces that Frank sandblasted look very different from those that he started with in the soda blasting photographs. They are, for the most part, much cleaner, because the soda blasting has rendered them free of paint and loose surface rust. This is one of the great advantages of Frank's two-step blasting routine. The first step cleans the metal surfaces and gives greatly improved visibility of the underlying metal. This allows Frank to see where best to concentrate the much higher energy of the sandblasting process.

As in the soda-blasting phase, Frank has positioned the cab and doors so that he has good access to every surface that he blasts. The jack stands under the cab ensure that he can easily direct his blast under it.

For sandblasting one of the doors, Frank uses the stand under it that he used when he soda blasted

9 *Blasting inside the cab raises a visible sand cloud. You can see why Frank wears a good respirator and very good eye, ear, and body protection. The visible stains in the right wheelwell cowl surface are tar, probably remnants of undercoating. You will get a closer look at them later.*

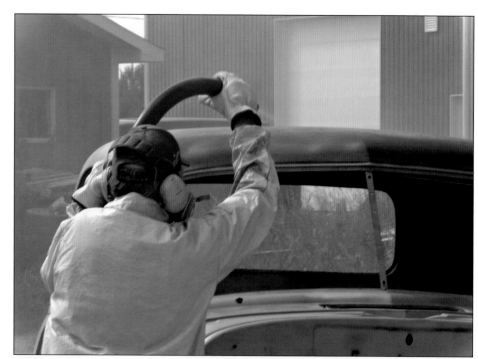

10 *Blasting the transition area in the front of the cab's roof, where compound curve gives way to flatter metal is tricky because it is easy to stretch and warp the flat metal. Note that Frank is using a relatively direct and close blast on the curved area.*

11 Frank has blasted the worst rust off the cab's roof and moved on to the underside of the cowl. He will return to the roof for final sandblasting later. In doing multiple blasting passes, Frank is able to better concentrate his attention on what is happening to the metal.

12 Having completed the soda and rough sand work on the cab's roof, Frank returns to finish the job. Note the very long distance and wide angle of his first, exploratory passes. This is flat metal that warps easily.

13 Frank has found a usable position for blasting the top of the roof. It isn't exactly comfortable, but it beats wobbling on a ladder. He needs the best possible visibility of the roof's surfaces. It is greatly to his advantage to stop blasting them the instant that they become clean.

14 As Frank blasts closer to his perch, he has to pull the nozzle back as far as he can. Even then, he ends up getting closer and closer to the metal that he is blasting. This means moving faster and being super observant of what is happening.

15 His perch through the cab's windshield has brought Frank uncomfortably close with his blast. He compensates for this by moving his nozzle faster. Fortunately, his closeness to the metal makes it easier for him to see the effects of his blast.

16 This door still looks pretty rusty after soda blasting, because the soda blast revealed metal that would be more efficiently dealt with by sandblasting. Given the amount of material removal required here, Frank used a long blast distance to minimize damage from long blasting exposure.

17 Frank attacked each door from many angles; this is key to removing heavy rust. Having the doors on the ground allowed him to do this easily by simply walking around them. It also increased his angle options.

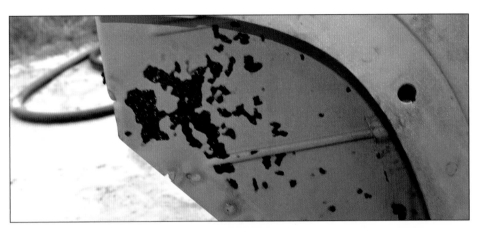

18 Between blasting the doors clean, Frank attacked some undercoating tar in the lower side-cowl surfaces of the car's wheelwells. They looked like this after soda; sandblasting also failed to remove the tar, because it was still soft and resilient.

19 Back on the door job, Frank turned to their inside panels. Little rust was here because the interior finish was still largely intact.

the doors. After starting to sand-blast the first door, he very quickly switched to placing the doors on pallets. This made it easier for him to maintain longer gun-to-target distances and acute attack angles. Small practical adjustments such as these are critical to preventing damage and getting the best possible results with sandblasting.

With his right knee and left leg through the cab's windshield pane holes while blasting the cab's roof, Frank exhibits the athleticism required to do great blasting work. Getting into the best position for what you are doing is extremely important, but can be difficult. This is work that is best done by hearty, agile individuals, although the rest of us can have our moments attempting it.

Unlike the bicarbonate of soda blasting, where the media breaks up and dissipates quickly as a fine dust, there is considerable blast back with sand, which is particularly noticeable when Frank is blasting the inside of the cab. The protective clothing and respiration filter that Frank was wearing made this process all the more uncomfortable. Although he was not under as severe a blast back assault as the metal that he was blasting, blast back always adds considerably to the difficulty of the task.

The small cover panel that Frank is seen cleaning on a pallet illustrates the importance of having everything ready to blast in as few sessions as possible. In this job, there were not a lot of separate, small parts, but in some jobs there can be many. It is much more efficient to do as much of your sand- and soda-blasting work at one time as is possible; and then follow up with the other necessary processes on the entire batch of parts.

20 *Frank employed a long blast distance to remove paint from the inside door surfaces. He used a very straight-on blast angle, because the paint yielded quickly to his blasting. With little need to dwell on any area very long, there was little chance of warping these panels.*

21 *A few stubborn stains around the stamped, flanged openings in the inner door panels required more dwell in those areas. Note that Frank is using a steeper blast angle to reach them.*

22 *The folded, crimped seams along the door skin edges are areas where all rust must be removed and the potential for warping is minimal. Frank worked his nozzle pretty close to these areas. Note that he is stabilizing the door from moving in reaction to his blast.*

23 *This job did not involve many small items. One of the few was the truck's battery cover. Frank blasted both of its sides on a pallet, always from a respectful distance.*

24 *As the cab wends its way back to Frank's shop, you notice traces of minor rust in a few areas. Most of it will be removed with Roloc abrasive discs (discussed earlier in this chapter) before painting. The remaining rust will be neutralized with a conditioning wash and/or etching primer.*

When the sandblasting work was finished, Frank transported the cab back to his shop for the next step in his stripping process. The parts look clean, but even after soda- and sand-blasting they are visibly not clear of all rust. This was not an oversight on Frank's part.

As a practical matter, it would be incredibly difficult, if not impossible, to remove all visible rust from this cab and doors with soda blasting and sandblasting alone. In areas such as the inside of the cab, this is also not necessary, because these areas will not be visible or exposed to most of the environmental factors that deteriorate finishes.

In the case of the highly visible interior and exterior exposed panels, Frank has removed almost all of the rust. This, alone, cannot guarantee paint adhesion for the long haul. Two additional steps are needed to get to that point. The next two steps in Frank's process (Step 4 and Step 5) make that guarantee

25 *If you are looking for absolute, molecular surface perfection, what they used to call "metallurgically clean," the result that you see here isn't even close. But in practical terms, with modern metal preps and reactive primers, it is better than serviceable for this job. Other jobs may require more.*

26 *The combination of natural and fluorescent light in Frank's shop certainly reveals all. Note that some of the stubborn tar on the cowl panel in the wheelwell remains. Scraping and applying solvents will remove it.*

27 *Although the metal in this cab had severe surface rust in many areas, close inspection of the blasted metal reveals no bulges, buckles, or warps. That is a definite plus.*

possible. First (Step 4) is to mechanically remove most of the rust that has survived soda and sandblasting and that might cause problems for long-term paint adhesion. Next (Step 5) is to apply a reactive (self-etching) primer to the cleaned metal to promote the adhesion of the sandable primer and topcoats that will be applied over the self-etching primer. The self-etching primer also protects the metal from flash rusting until the final finish coats can be applied.

The point to remember is that while absolutely clean metal is always desirable, it may not always be practically attainable. To try to get there with Frank's soda and sandblasting sequence is not practical, because it would almost inevitably result in damage to the metal. By adding these post-blasting

28 *An outside photograph of the right door shows what the surface of the blasted metal looks like. It provides a good profile for primer adhesion and a good basis for a finish. This surface needs little dinging work or filler.*

29 *Although all of the inside surfaces of the cab are far from being rust free, those that will be seen are easily clean enough to hold a finish without problems. The unseen surfaces can be treated with conditioners, etching primers, or urethane paints and will never yield to rusting.*

steps, Frank attains a practical compromise that will protect his work for generations.

For example, if you raise the blast pressure or media particle size to a point where you see evidence of warping, you have to increase the gun-to-target distance or pass speed to compensate for those changes. Those are the fast countermeasures that you can take to avoid damage. You could also lower your blast pressure or use a larger blast nozzle for the same result.

But, of course, you are not a computer that can calculate these variables and the appropriate countermeasures as they change. It would be difficult to optimize all of the blast variables. In fact, many combinations of factors could be optimal. Even a master abrasive blaster such as Frank Weinert cannot compute them to a specific, exact, and correct result. What he can do is use his experience and observational powers to achieve that result. For Frank, this is like an instinct. When he senses or observes the early evidence of damage from putting too much blast energy into a panel, or area of a panel, he instinc-

tively makes a correction before damage occurs. With experience, you can develop the same skill set. It is, for the most part, a matter of learned restraint.

It is almost needless to say, but it is a good idea to learn the sheet-metal blast stripping craft by taking some scrap panels and seeing what kinds of blast applications they do and do not tolerate before they begin to warp. A couple of days of this kind of self-education can make you proficient at safe blasting without risking treasured panels.

It is always tempting to go after an area, or a speck, or a pit of rust that resists sandblasting by focusing a little extra blast on it until it disappears. That means putting just a little more energy into the metal. It's a natural thing to do and can be done by dwell-

ing your blast on that speck or pit just a little longer than on the surrounding metal, or coming in a little closer with your nozzle, or hitting it with a slightly more perpendicular blast angle. Sadly, with an aggressive cutting media, such as the quartz sand that Frank uses, such a seemingly small addition of blasting energy can maim or kill what he is blasting.

Unfortunately, you can damage or even destroy a panel quickly if you succumb to the natural human temptation to complete your entire cleaning task while you are there with your sandblast stream.

It takes judgment and restraint to know when to quit. The best time to quit is before you damage a panel badly or irreparably.

Frank knows this because he has had a lot of experience repairing

This surface was blasted with soda and sand, but some corrosion remained, and some occurred after blasting. Here, Frank is removing it mechanically with a drill-motor-mounted Roloc abrasive wheel. Although this process is slow, it allows Frank to apply abrasive action in a very controlled and visible manner.

metal and blasting it. He knows metal's limits with regard to how much blasting energy it can absorb before it succumbs to damage that can be very difficult to repair. And he always stops short of the point of doing that damage.

As Frank moved from the soda-blasting phase of stripping the cab and doors of the subject truck to the sandblasting phase, he had to be intently watchful for signs of blasting damage. The soda-blasting phase did not present these problems because soda is too mild a media to do any real damage to sheet metal. Frank's nozzle distances were much greater for sandblasting than for soda blasting. His blast pressure remained the same (90 psi), as did his nozzle size (half an inch). Everything else changed, not just his nozzle distance. His maximum dwell time, his overall pass speed, and his blast angle had to be adjusted to the harder and sharper sand media that he was now using. Frank knows that quartz sand is as unforgiving as soda is tolerant.

Step 4 is to mechanically abrade remaining corrosion from areas where it survived the abrasive blasting processes in Step 2 and Step 3. Think of this as Frank's search-and-destroy mission. Any deep rust pit tends to contain enough moisture to continue its corrosion process, even under most "moisture impermeable" coatings, such as self-etching primers. Although that type of primer and several types of metal conditioners successfully deal with very small rust inclusions, it is best to remove as many of them as is practical.

Frank's basic weapon against the kinds of rust spots and pits that may successfully evade his blasting processes is to use drill-driven 2-inch 3M Scotch-Brite Roloc wheels, or their equivalent. He uses a coarse grade of this type of abrasive mesh wheel, rotating it with a drill motor. This gives him excellent control in attacking resistant rust spots and pits, as well as small, deeply rusted areas. Using these discs can be slow, but avoids gouging and overheating damage to metal. In most cases, the areas to be dealt with are pretty small.

Frank's final procedure is to blow all surfaces and other areas clean with compressed air (Step 5) and then to apply a self-etching primer (also known as "reactive primer") to the surfaces that Frank cleaned (Frank's

The 3M Scotch-Brite Roloc abrasive system, a variant of which is shown here, uses an easy to install and replace wheel that contains powerful abrasive in a mesh matrix. The coarse grade wheel, shown here, is ideal for spot corrosion removal.

Advantages of the Roloc abrasive system include its simplicity and convenience. The discs are expensive, between $1 and $2 each, but they last a long time and can be driven with an inexpensive drill motor. They also change out very easily and quickly.

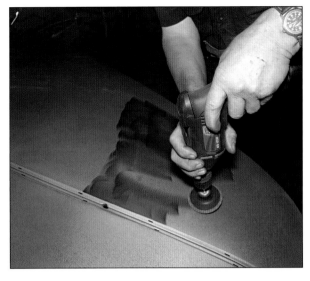

Although Frank would ordinarily reblast this hood, he is demonstrating here that the Roloc-type abrasive system is capable of removing deep corrosion and can move along quite quickly. No one would seriously advocate stripping an entire car this way, but it is great for spot rust removal.

Step 1 through Frank's Step 4). Frank does this as quickly as possible after finishing the cleaning phases of his work, to prevent corrosion from continuing or restarting on the cleaned surfaces.

Before the invention of modern self-etching epoxy primers, various metal conditioners and converters were used to protect freshly cleaned sheet metal and to provide adhesion for the primer and finish coats applied over bare metal. These formulations were usually based on phosphoric acid, or sometimes on other acids, and worked by etching cleaned surfaces slightly and converting them to a more stable chemistry that would resist rust better than bare metal.

Ford popularized this type of process on its vehicles almost 100 years ago. Various versions of it have persisted to the present. Aftermarket variants of Ford's phosphatizing process are based on similar chemistry.

Although metal conditioners and converters are still used to treat raw metal before painting it, the more modern practice is to employ self-etching primers, probably because they do a much better job than the older metal conditioners and converters.

Frank uses a reactive primer, PPG DP50 LF. This type of product has many advantages over the old metal conditioners and converters. It is much easier to spray onto a surface than it is to work with the wipe, wait, and wipe regimen required with the old conditioner/converter products. It is also much easier to make its application consistent. It does everything that the older products did, and much more.

Essentially, modern self-etching primers react with the base metal to which they are applied and bond strongly to it. This reduces the need for a somewhat rough metal surface to promote primer adhesion. A second advantage of modern, self-etching primers is that they are extremely waterproof. Unlike sanding primers, which are porous and only slightly waterproof, self-etching primers are dense enough to resist the transit of water molecules through them. They offer superior protection for raw metal until it can be primed with sanding primer layers and topcoat finishes.

After Frank has completed spraying the cleaned metal of the GM cab and doors with PPG DP50 LF, they can be stored safely for weeks before they are primed and top coated.

On the right are Frank's equipment essentials for doing the kind of soda and sandblasting work that you see on the left: a 385 SCFM diesel rotary-screw compressor, an air dryer, and valving to send air to his soda pot or sandblast pot (not visible).

Frank's Soda- and Sandblasting Equipment

Frank's equipment for both soda and sandblasting uses a 385 SCFM Ingersoll-Rand rotary screw diesel compressor coupled to an air drying unit. The drying unit is necessary to remove moisture from the heated air output of the compressor. This prevents condensation from forming in the plumbing to the blast pot, in the pot's mixing valve, and in the blast hose, as the compressed air's temperature drops.

Frank designed his system so that it could be converted from soda-blast media to sandblast media by changing the positions of two valves. Both systems use the same hose and nozzle. The soda-blasting pot is a 2-cubic-foot unit and holds almost enough soda to do the job described and shown in this chapter without refilling. Only one minor addition of soda to the pot was required to finish soda blasting the cab and doors.

The considerably larger sandblast pot that Frank uses looks like it came through a war on the losing side, but it blasts like a champ. Sandblasting is a rough abrasive process. How well equipment works has little to do with how it looks. Simpler equipment is often more rugged and reliable than pretty equipment. As long as blasting equipment is reliable and large enough to do the job, the real basis for high-quality and efficient work is primarily the skill and experience of the blast operator. Although I've met slicker talkers than Frank Weinert, I have yet to meet anyone who produces better results than he does. And, I've met many sandblast operators who don't come close to Frank's results.

This Ingersoll-Rand mobile diesel compressor is the heart of Frank's abrasive blasting operations. It produces more than enough air to feed the no. 5 (1/2-inch) blast nozzle that he uses for both soda and sandblasting, and is very reliable. It is also quite economical to run for what it does.

Frank's entire soda-blasting outfit is reasonably compact and self-contained. It is ideally sized for the work that he is doing and performs its job reliably. I have seen larger, fancier, and shinier blasting equipment, but I doubt if it would work any better than this setup for Frank's jobs.

The condensing-air drying unit in the center of the photograph removes moisture from the compressor's output air. The dryer can be plumbed to the soda-blast pot on its right, or to Frank's sandblast pot. The pots mix abrasive with air in specified proportions and deliver it to the blast nozzle.

Flipping a two-ball valve allows Frank to convert his blast from soda to sand, using the same blast hose and nozzle. This is a definite advantage in his work. Completely separate soda and sand systems might be desirable for some jobs, but not for stripping automotive sheet metal.

You are looking at a job well done. The outside of this body is almost perfectly clean. What little contamination remains will be removed mechanically. The interior of the cab is as clean as it needs to be. Most interior areas will be covered by upholstery and trim.

Frank's blast pot doesn't look like much, but it gets the job done. This is a very simple setup that performs well and gives little trouble beyond an occasional clog in the air/media mixing valve. Great abrasive blasting work is more a matter of operator skill than fancy equipment.

CHOOSING ABRASIVE BLASTING MATERIALS

Because of the dizzying array of abrasive blasting materials available, the question quickly arises, "Which is the best one?" Inevitably the answer is, "It depends on what you're trying to accomplish and what your resources are." Having stated the obvious, let's now look at the main factors in choosing the best blasting media for your job.

Oh, and as Detective Columbo used to say, "Just one more thing . . ." Although I will discuss the use of various abrasives as blasting media, some of what I say about them applies as well to their use on abrasive papers, discs, meshes, and other mechanical application vehicles. In some cases, it also applies to them as media for tumbling and vibratory cleaning operations.

In choosing a blasting media, think about what you are blasting, what kind of system you are using, and what you are attempting to accomplish with abrasive blasting. It is best to boil these and other variables down to the essential media selections that they mandate. I will do that first, with six considerations in choosing blasting media.

Blasting can be done in a contained cabinet or room, or outside with no recovery and/or recycling. It can be done with full pressure equipment or suction equipment. Dozens of variables can factor into blasting situations; despite this, I can refine six factors into one point of decision in choosing the best media for a situation and job.

Consideration 1: Recycling Potential

Whether or not media will be recovered and processed for recycling is always a consideration. It is relevant whether you are using a siphon system or a pressure system and whether you are blasting inside a cabinet or blast booth or in the great outdoors.

You are looking at five samples of useful abrasive blasting media. From left to right: plastic blasting media, garnet, steel grit, aluminum oxide, and glass bead. I'm not sure if much can be learned from looking at blasting media samples, except that they usually look quite different from each other. (Photo Courtesy Clemco Industries)

What you are blasting makes a difference in your choice of blasting media. Areas of deep rust make this frame a prime candidate for sand media blasting. Before it is blasted with sand, it is lightly soda blasted to remove any grease or oil that escaped steam cleaning.

Consideration 2: Blast Damage Potential

How robust or delicate is the item you are blasting? Obviously, blasting a steel vehicle frame has very different media requirements than blasting a fiberglass fender or an aluminum engine part. The qualification for media used to blast a body or panel stripped of all glass and trim versus one that is fully assembled and dressed with trim is significant. Some media attacks the surfaces of items such as glass and plastic trim, while other, less aggressive, media do not.

Consideration 3: Material Type

This factor is related directly to media aggressiveness. Removing a manmade coating is different from removing rust, because rust is usually better adhered than most finishes and is often pitted deeply into the substrate. Different coatings can present very different blast removal propositions and levels of difficulty. More aggressive media, that is, media that is harder and sharper, tend to be more effective in removing stubborn contaminants such as rust, powder coating, epoxy coating, etc. A few exceptions do exist to this rule of thumb.

These parts are perfect candidates for soda blasting. The aluminum alloy carburetor riser (left) and fuel vaporizer (center) are delicate and will benefit from soda's gentle cleaning power. The hubcap (right) is nickel-plated brass. Soda blasting and polishing may refurbish it and avoid having to plate it.

In this regard, it is interesting to note that soft coatings are often much more difficult and/or time consuming to blast successfully than harder coatings. This is because they tend to bounce blasting media off with minimal damage to the coating. Generally, harder coatings are more brittle and can be fractured by blasting media as the first step in removing them. Soft coatings may have to be stretched and hardened by blasting before they yield.

Consideration 4: Surface Goal

The steps you'll take after blasting significantly influence your choice of media. Does your blasted surface need to be slightly rough to promote mechanical primer adhesion, or can it be very smooth and rely solely on a chemical metal conditioning or reactive primer for adhesion? How quickly will the surface be protected from corrosion after it is blasted? How smooth do you want the surface to be after it is coated, and how much priming and sanding are you willing to do to get what you want? The answers to these questions and more relate directly to media composition, particle size and shape—all the factors that determine the aggressiveness of the media.

Consideration 5: Media Cost

Cost can be difficult to calculate. More recyclable media usually are more expensive to buy than less recyclable media on a cost-per-pound basis. Factors such as equipment wear also enter into media cost, as does the effect of media choice on the time that it takes to blast various coatings and types of surfaces.

Bicarbonate of soda is a one-trip media because it breaks up too completely for recycling. It lacks aggressiveness, but still has a major place in automotive blasting. Soda doesn't threaten delicate surfaces and it removes paint and loose rust economically, making it great for revealing "what lies beneath." Larger particle sizes work best. (Photo Courtesy The Eastwood Company)

Silicon carbide is an extremely sharp-edged, hard, and dense media. It's very reclaimable and cuts extremely quickly, but it also can warp or cut through metal quickly. The 60- to 80-grit sizes are preferred for general automotive work. Silicon carbide is a relatively expensive blasting media. (Photo Courtesy The Eastwood Company)

Aluminum oxide is probably the best all-around, reclaimable automotive blasting media. Its cost is typically half that of silicon carbide. Grit sizes that are between 50 and 90 work best. I have found that aluminum oxide blasting residues can interfere with soldering, brazing, and welding on steel surfaces. (Photo Courtesy The Eastwood Company)

The costs of various media not only vary greatly between different media types, but also can depend largely on how near to, or far from, their sources you are. For example, slag media such as coal slag and cold chilled copper slag are byproducts of industrial processes that exist in very specific locations. Their costs, all graded, bagged, and shipped to your location, may depend largely on how far you are from where they are produced; their value can be largely the cost of the freight and handling to get them to you. This is particularly true of mineral media and industrial refuse byproduct media, such as silica sand and coal slag.

Of course, the ability to recycle enters into cost. A one-way media, such as bicarbonate of soda, may seem cheap by the pound but expensive to use when you consider that it only serves for one trip through your blast system. In the case of soda, good equipment that effectively minimizes soda use is the key to keeping the cost low.

Media that are recyclable through a system may have very different durabilities for reuse, from a few cycles to many. The reuse potential figures largely in calculating the cost

of a media. The cycle costs of various media can include multiple other expenses as well.

Some blasting media types, carbon dioxide or dry ice, for example, defy most common categories of consideration. Carbon dioxide is inexpensive to acquire or to create, it leaves the scene on its own with no disposal issues or expenses, and it is safe in almost any regard. It would seem to be the ideal blasting media, and it is for some applications. Unfortunately, it is not at all aggressive, so beyond removing grease, superficial surface soils, and very loose corrosion products, its applications are quite limited. In other words, for most purposes it passes a couple of the five categories perfectly, but it flunks the cost consideration almost completely because the time it would take to remove deep rust with it would be terribly long. It also flunks Consideration 3 (Material Type) because of the short list of contaminants that it can remove.

Finally, with regard to cost, some media have different equipment requirements than others. That is a definite cost factor. Equipment maintenance is another element of this category. Soft media, such as the plastic media and soda, do little or no damage to equipment, while others such as tungsten carbide, aluminum oxide, and garnet may require relatively frequent replacement of perishable system parts, such as mixing valves and blast nozzles, among other expensive possibilities.

Consideration 6: Health and Safety

Media choices must consider health and safety factors. These factors can be quite complex and variable, depending on the type and condition

Ground (fractured, crushed, and bottle) glass media are similar to silica sand in blasting characteristics, but without the silicosis hazard associated with sand media. This is a relatively inexpensive media sold in grades from roughly 8 to 80 mesh. It is not recyclable. The larger grades are best for automotive work. (Photo Courtesy The Eastwood Company)

of the equipment that you use, the safety measures that you take, what you are blasting, and the frequency and length of your exposure to any hazards created by a particular blast media. Therefore, only general conclusions make sense for health and safety.

By now many people are aware of silicosis, a deadly lung disease that can result from exposure to the airborne silicon associated with sandblasting and other industrial processes. Although opinions vary regarding the level of exposure that is dangerous, it is safe to say that as knowledge of this disease increases, we learn that the level of exposure considered dangerous is less today than it was two decades ago, a decade ago, five years ago, etc.

Another example in the health and safety category is the use of agricultural media in closed blasting systems. This class includes media such as cornstarch, corncobs, rice, walnut shells, etc. In some situations these media have the potential for creating spontaneous combustion explosions; albeit the possibilities of this happening are remote. Although spontaneous combustion has become a consideration for industry, it hardly concerns someone with a small tumbler filled with walnut shell media, or a small vibratory device filled with parts and pulverized peach pit media.

Safety and health implications should be a serious consideration in your choice of media. Make a point of reading safety warnings on media containers and researching the hazards of each media. Then, act on that knowledge.

Summary of Factors

In sum, these six considerations form the basis for making good media selection decisions: (1) potential for recyclability, (2) potential for blast damage, (3) what you are trying to remove from what you are blasting, (4) what kind of surface you want to leave when your blasting is finished, (5) media cost, and (6) media health and safety factors. Other factors may be important, too, in making your blasting media choices.

For example, media particle size can, in many cases, be specified. Larger particles impart more energy to blast targets, other factors being equal. That can make them more effective and/or more potentially damaging to thin sections. Particle size is definitely a factor to consider when choosing abrasive blast media. Consultation with media sellers and independent research sources, and experience, will help to inform you on particle size decisions. In the case of some media, such as glass bead, particle size makes a huge difference in results because it greatly affects the surface characteristics of what you are blasting.

To continue this example, some media tend to be poorly sorted by particle size, to the point that they can cause equipment problems. Others may leave residues that can cause issues with the surfaces that you blast; poor paint adhesion is an example. But these problems tend to

Glass bead is a peening media that's great for cleaning engine parts and castings because it doesn't cut into surfaces and changes the blasting subject's dimensions very little. The finest glass bead grades (100 and up) work best. Glass beaded surfaces require an etching primer or other measures to provide good paint adhesion. (Photo Courtesy The Eastwood Company)

Pulverized walnut shells are both tumbling and blasting media. Grades range from 6/10 to 40/100 mesh, and beyond. This is a soft media that removes very loose contamination with almost no potential for damaging metal. In tumbling applications, it is typically used with a liquid abrasive for polishing soft metals. (Photo Courtesy The Eastwood Company)

be both sporadic and soluble. The six main considerations, noted above, should get you started on making good blast media choices.

My Favorite Abrasives

The following is a list with brief notes on various abrasive types for blasting, tumbling, and vibrating.

Agricultural Abrasives

In my experience, none of the "agricultural abrasives" do much for blasting body panels or most mechanical parts. Walnut shells, cornstarch, corncobs, rice, milo, and various and assorted shredded and pulverized fruit pit abrasives may work well in some tumbling or vibratory applications, but have little relevance to abrasive blasting to achieve clean metal. At best, they are polishing media when used on metal parts. In most cases, they fail to satisfy the requirements of Consideration 3 (Material Type) and can be rejected for stripping painted and rusted metal on that basis alone.

Mineral Abrasives

Mineral abrasives are the mainline media for stripping paint and rust from metal. These media can be used alone or in tandem with other media. Sometimes they are used with enhancers and additives. In any form, they outperform most other abrasives in this category of work. Most mineral abrasives do not cause excessive dust problems in contained blasting situations and provide good visibility of the item you are blasting.

The best-known mineral abrasives are sands of various descriptions. That is why abrasive blasting is often loosely called "sandblasting," to the great annoyance of people who sell non-sand abrasives. Silica and quartz describe blasting sands generally, but within those classifications are tremendous variations. In my opinion, silica and quartz sands are the best bet for most automotive stripping because they get full passes on all considerations when they are used in contained systems or with reasonable health and safety precautions for outside blasting.

Obviously, there are health concerns about the safety of using sand abrasives for outside blasting. These concerns depend largely on the level of exposure and the safety equipment that a blaster employs. You should consider the safety of every abrasive that you use in making your decision to use it. Fractured bottle glass is similar to sand in terms of its strengths and potential weakness.

Silica-containing abrasives become safer when used in tandem with non-silica-containing abrasives, such as soda and plastic media. The simple reason for this is that using combinations such as soda, and then silica sand, means you do the bulk of your blasting without sand, greatly reducing your exposure to airborne silica.

Slag Byproducts

Slag byproducts are popular for abrasive blasting and succeed in almost every consideration category, with a few reservations. Their recycle cost, Consideration 1 (Recycling Potential) can be quite variable. They can also leave smudgy residues if they are not properly processed. Finally, they are sometimes poorly graded and can cause clogging in some abrasive blasting equipment. Depending on your application, they are often very much on a par with sand abrasives in their cost and effectiveness, although they tend to be harder on equipment. Slag byproducts are generally safer to use than sand abrasives because they do not have the same potential to cause silicosis.

Garnet and Aluminum Oxide

Garnet and aluminum oxide are very good blast abrasives but tend to be expensive compared to sand, so much so that they are poor choices if they cannot be recovered and recycled, Consideration 1 (Recycling Potential). They are fine cabinet and blast room blasting media, but I don't recommend using them where recovery and recycling are not possible.

Baking Soda

Bicarbonate of soda (baking soda) is a great media for removing paint and loose rust, and it is environmentally and health neutral. Although it cannot be recycled, it is inexpensive enough to use on a lost abrasive basis if you have equipment that meters it properly. Unfortunately, a lot of equipment does a poor job of metering soda. This can make it unreasonably expensive to use. Equipment that does meter soda efficiently can be quite expensive to acquire.

Used alone, soda fails Consideration 5 (Media Cost) for most automotive panel work. However, when used in a two-stage blasting regimen, that is, soda followed by sand or by another more-aggressive mineral blasting media, soda is efficient and results in very high-quality work. It is also extremely effective for cleaning mechanical parts, particularly alloys of aluminum and magnesium, when material removal and dimensional change must be kept at a minimum. I wouldn't clean aluminum pistons or cylinder heads with anything else. Soda is one of the few media that is aggressive enough to do serious surface cleaning while presenting virtually no risk of warping or distorting thin sections, such as very delicate alloy body panels.

Soda is my first choice where coatings, and not rust, are the issue. It is amazingly capable of removing a wide variety of coatings. It is also the perfect way to clean aluminum for coating or welding. Finally, I sometimes use it when I am not sure that I have removed all grease and oil from a complex part or structure. The soda tends to remove it or, in some cases, stick to it. This tells me when a job will benefit from additional solvent or steam cleaning before further blasting is attempted.

Glass and Ceramic Bead

Glass and ceramic bead are wonderfully useful for cleaning mechanical parts but are too expensive to use if they cannot be recycled. They pass Consideration 1 (Recycling Potential) brilliantly. If you have the equipment to effectively separate and recycle these media, then they can pass Consideration 3 (Material Type).

Although ceramic bead is quite expensive (more expensive than glass bead), it is one of the most durable and useful media in existence for cleaning thicker items with minimal material removal. However, either bead would be a poor choice of media for general paint and rust removal work, particularly on sheet metal. Both of these bead types are peening media, not cutting media, and have considerable potential for warping thin sections. However, glass bead is an excellent media for cleaning steel and iron mechanical parts, including engine parts.

Steel shot has similar characteristics to glass bead. It is a peening media that works best when it is mechanically generated. In that capacity, it is excellent for cleaning steel and iron mechanical parts, but the equipment to generate it for blasting purposes is extremely expensive. Steel grit can be air blasted to clean fairly heavy metal sections but is overkill for sheet metal and can actually murder it.

Plastic media blasting (PMB) was on the road to becoming popular about 20 or 30 years ago. The media to perform PMB were basically recycled and reground thermoset plastics, including styrene. Urea-formaldehyde, acrylic, and polyester plastics are now commonly used for PMB applications.

PMB went off the road to popularity after a few years because people began to notice that it was a fairly slow way to remove paint and did little to remove rust. Its advantages were in the areas of Consideration 1 (Recycling Potential), Consideration 5 (Media Cost), and Consideration 6 (Health and Safety). Its main weakness was in the area of Consideration 3 (Material Type). With that realization, its popularity for automotive blasting declined. In many instances soda blasting replaced PMB because soda was more effective and usually less expensive to use. Still, some applications for PMB remain.

Other specialty blasting abrasives (and many exist) are generally indicated for specific requirements in highly specified industrial applications. Leading abrasive suppliers' websites provide further information on blasting media and its best applications.

ABRASIVE BLASTING EQUIPMENT, SUPPLIES AND ACCESSORIES

Abrasive blasting has been around for more than a hundred years. In that time, thousands of manufacturers have developed enormous varieties of equipment, supplies, and accessories to support it. Some of that equipment and those supplies and accessories worked well, and some didn't. By now, most of what is on the market works pretty well. Not as many manufacturers of blasting equipment, supplies, and accessories are in business now as in the past, but you still have a substantial choice in this field.

Roughly speaking, new blasting equipment and accessories fall into two categories, light to medium consumer equipment and accessories and medium- to heavy-duty industrial equipment and accessories. Industrial equipment and accessories tend to be inherently heavy-duty and much more expensive than consumer-grade blasting paraphernalia. Personally, I have six industrial blast cabinets, two industrial reclaim/pressure pot systems, and one industrial pressure pot with a separate dust collector. I also have

three consumer-level pressure pots. This equipment profile gives me the equipment that I need to do most of the abrasive blasting jobs that I am called on to perform.

If you are new to blasting, I recommend that you look at both kinds of equipment, light consumer and medium- to heavy-duty commercial/industrial. The latter inevitably costs much more when it is purchased new. However, it is often available in decent used condition at very reasonable

This large industrial Clemco classic pot system features robust construction and advanced features, such as the blow-off muffler at its top that reduces noise when the pot is depressurized. Remote pressure controls and a mixing valve designed to reduce wear make this a great blasting pot for large jobs. (Photo Courtesy Clemco Industries)

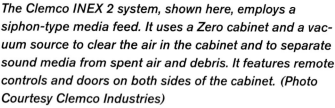

The Clemco INEX 2 system, shown here, employs a siphon-type media feed. It uses a Zero cabinet and a vacuum source to clear the air in the cabinet and to separate sound media from spent air and debris. It features remote controls and doors on both sides of the cabinet. (Photo Courtesy Clemco Industries)

Clemco designates the Zero BNP 6012 013 as a "mini blast room." Its blast area is almost 5 feet x 5 feet and a tad over 4 feet tall. It can be fitted with a variety of pressure pots and dust collector options and is designed for continuous operation with a variety of abrasives. (Photo Courtesy Clemco Industries)

prices. Both new light-duty blasting equipment and used industrial/commercial equipment have distinct advantages and disadvantages.

Industrial/Commercial Blasting Equipment

All photos in this section are courtesy of Clemco Industries.

Industrial and commercial compressors are almost always justified for blasting equipment. Although a detailed discussion of compressors is beyond the scope of this book, two points must be made about compressors used for abrasive blast-

ing. The first is that any compressor that you acquire is likely to quickly become too small for your needs. This is one place where "Think Big" always works best. I consider a 5-hp compressor marginal for most small blasting equipment setups.

My second point about compressors is that only high-quality compressors deliver clean air reliably. Inexpensive consumer-grade compressors lack the design features and quality construction to support serious abrasive blasting on more than an occasional basis. That may be fine if you are an occasional blaster, but bad if your demands are greater than that.

Combined, my two points

strongly suggest that if you want to do any serious abrasive blasting, you would do well to buy the biggest and best compressor that your circumstances permit. It will probably save you money in the medium and long runs. It will also save you the frustration and grief of working with equipment that is too small and/or too weak to keep up with your demands for air and to support what you are doing.

While we're thinking BIG in the commercial/industrial realm, photos of very large, industrial Clemco equipment, such as those items shown above might inspire us. Clemco, in Washington, Missouri, is the world's largest manufacturer and

This is what the inside of a blast room looks like. The item under blast attack is too large to fit into a blast cabinet, leaving outside blasting or a blast room as the only options for blasting it. The operator is breathing outside air and is protected from blast, head to toe.

In this view of a blast room operation, a group of small parts has replaced the large item in the last photograph. In this case, they could have been moved into and out of a large cabinet, but the efficiency of blasting them all at once in a batch is apparently preferable.

seller of abrasive blasting equipment and enjoys a reputation for design, quality, and reliability that is second to none.

Clemco's product line includes many "latest idea" innovations in areas such as sealing, cabinet durability, cabinet visibility, pressure pot control, blast nozzles, and much more. Clemco equipment also provides extensive customization services to fit industrial needs. Customized systems can be ordered to deal with the unique and specific requirements of a wide range of industrial jobs.

Clemco makes blasting enclosures as big as blast rooms. These can be rooms big enough to contain very large machinery, with plenty of room to get around it. Of course, blast rooms are beyond the needs of most automotive work. Still, if you want to do all-weather stripping of bodies and frames, a blast room might be just the ticket for you.

At the other end of Clemco's vast product line is the Zero BNP 55 5 blast cabinet. I have a soft spot in my heart for this model because, for nearly 40 years, I've owned a predecessor Zero cabinet that is very much like it. It was my second cabinet purchase and has been a faithful performer, quietly and efficiently doing every job that I sent into it without incident or complaint. Total maintenance on this cabinet has been three window replacements and a mixing valve diaphragm replacement. That's all. Note that the contemporary BNP 55 5 has some greatly updated features from my version and is packaged with a simple cyclone separator that reclaims recyclable media from spent abrasive fragments and blast-created debris.

Reclaimers, such as the one mounted on the back of the Zero

Think of this mobile Clemco blast room as a kind of spray booth for blasting. Note its very heavy construction and the provisions for collecting the spent blast through its grated floor. Note also the ample overhead lighting and the provision of a side door for the operator.

The CLECO BNP 55 5 blasting cabinet features a work area 42 inches wide, 23 inches deep, and 30 inches high. It comes packaged with a reclaimer and can be ordered with a dust bag or dust collector ancillary unit. Packaged here for suction blasting, this unit looks ideal for a small automotive shop.

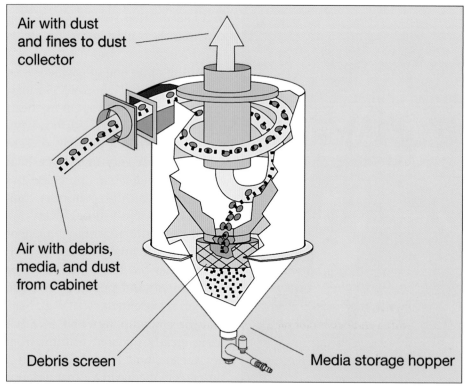

Air with dust and fines to dust collector

Air with debris, media, and dust from cabinet

Debris screen

Media storage hopper

This illustration of the reclaimer (included with the Clemco BNP 55 5 Zero cabinet) reveals the principle of operation by a centrifugal reclaimer (cyclone separator). It uses centrifugal force to separate heavier sound media from lighter air and spent media, as well as from blast debris.

BNP 55 5, vary in size and sophistication, but they all employ the same basic principle, centrifugal force, to separate sound media from dust and debris. Dust and debris tend to be lighter and less dense than sound media.

In practice, reclaimers use a large radial blade fan to drive and accelerate media around a dished circular ramp. The heavier particles (sound media) descend the bowl ramp rapidly and fall through a hole in its dished bottom into a separate containment area at the base of the reclaim unit. Dust and debris are lighter and less dense than sound media, so they move faster and exit

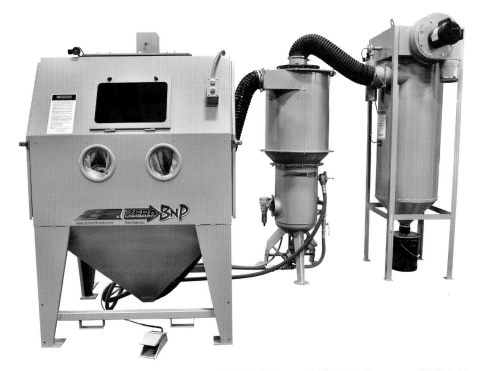

The highly sophisticated and customizable Clemco BNP 220 Pressure CDC 013 Zero Cabinet system has a work area 50 inches wide, 39 inches deep, and 43 inches high. Equipped as shown here, it features two doors and is hooked to a reclaimer-over-pressure pot system that is attached to a second reclaiming unit.

The Clemco Pulsar IX-P 11 modular cabinet system comes as one unit, complete with a dust collector on top of a pressure pot. In the modular configuration shown here, it features innovative features such as an adjustable vortex reclaimer and a self-purging media filter pair with replaceable cartridges.

the bowl with waste air at a higher ramp level. These smaller, lighter particles can then be filtered from the air that is carrying them and removed from the system.

On a far grander scale is the Clemco BNP 220 Pressure CDC 013 blast cabinet, pressure pot, and two-stage dust collector ensemble. Its huge cabinet has many automated features. Note that it is paired with a reclaim unit mounted on top of a pressure pot. It also features a second reclaim unit for two-stage separation. This type of setup guarantees extremely clean operation, with little or no emission of waste blast products from the system into the environment.

The Clemco IX-P 11 is a large modular unit with an integrated reclaim unit and pressure pot. As the pressure pot cycles (on operator command) between pressurized and depressurized conditions, a large poppet valve at its top opens and closes. In the open part of this cycle, the accumulated reclaimed media in the reclaim unit's base containment area drops into the pressure pot. When the operator resumes blasting, the pressure pot, now containing the reclaimed media, is repressurized.

Clemco also manufactures and sells a complete line of siphon systems and blast hoppers for situations that do not require pressure blasting. These range from small to huge and include various types of controls and features. Some have extraordinary features, such as the Wetblast FLEX, for example, which is capable of vapor or slurry blasting. Those terms describe blasting with a combination of media and liquid vapor (usually water) mixed in varying proportions.

The difference between Clemco's wet-blasting systems and some

This Clemco 1028 pressure blast pot has only 1/2 cubic foot of media capacity. It blasts that load in about 15 minutes through a 3/8-inch nozzle, running at 80 psi. Its portability makes it ideal for switching between multiple cabinets, with added potential for small outside blasting jobs.

The Clemco Model 1642 isn't as portable as the 1028 but at 2 cubic feet it has four times the capacity. It will also blast for about 15 minutes at 80 psi, but through a 5/16-inch nozzle. That means a wider blast pattern and better productivity.

Clemco's Wetblast Flex machine injects liquid at the nozzle or blast hose base. A 6-cubic-foot blast pot and 120-gallon liquid tank give it good blasting capacity. The whole system is modular and very portable, making it perfect for small wet-blasting projects. It looks simple and durable, too.

others on the market is that Clemco's units run the liquid separately from the solid media; the liquid, in an atomized format, is combined with the solid media near the output nozzle. Some other manufacturers attempt to run the solid and liquid media together through a blast pot. This can raise all kinds of durability and maintenance issues. Solid abrasive media and water do not coexist well inside a pressurized blast pot, where they can cause lots of problems with a pot's inner surfaces and metering mechanisms.

Clemco also sells superior soda-blasting equipment under its Aerolyte Bicarbonator brand. If you have been frustrated by inexpensive and inferior soda-blasting equipment, you might want to take a look at Clemco's offerings. In particular, Clemco features high-quality blast

These are a few of Clemco's silicon carbide–lined Venturi blast nozzles. Note that they differ in Venturi length, bore, and mounting base type, among other variations. Clemco makes thousands (literally) of nozzle applications to cover virtually every blasting situation. The rubberized outer casings are designed to protect the nozzle.

cabinets with air extraction systems that disperse overblast from the immediate blast area (ClearView Ventilation Technology) and allow the operator to see with great clarity what he or she is blasting.

These systems also feature sophisticated and specialized blast pots and nozzles that have been developed for the express purpose of soda blasting. Among other advantages, these pots and nozzles can greatly reduce the amount of soda required to perform specific jobs. In almost all cases, this dramatically reduces the overall cost of soda-blasting jobs.

Like compressors, blast nozzles are an extremely important factor in successful blasting outcomes. The performance difference between an el cheapo steel or ceramic nozzle and

Clemco tungsten carbide–lined nozzles, such as those shown here, are legendary in the field of abrasive blasting. Great nozzles such as these increase productivity because they are durable and highly efficient in producing maximum blast effect for the air that is consumed. Good nozzles are critical to successful blasting.

a well-designed professional nozzle made with advanced materials can be huge. Efficiently designed nozzles made of superior materials can accelerate your blast stream. This increases blasting speed while reducing job time. In addition, it often reduces media consumption. That adds up to improved efficiency. Lining nozzles with advanced materials such as silicon carbide, tungsten carbide, or boron carbide guarantees that they maintain their superiority for hundreds, or thousands, of blasting hours with most media.

A great nozzle is not just a short piece of pipe or other material. It is a highly engineered structure with the consideration of many advanced and subtle factors inherent in its design and manufacture.

Clemco blast nozzles are industry-leading units, available in an incredibly wide variety of configurations, sizes, and material types. Advanced venturi-effect designs that accelerate air/media output velocities complement advanced nozzle materials and reduce wear on nozzle surfaces. At the other extreme, soda-blast nozzles, for example, do not require very hard inner surfaces because soda is a non-aggressive media. These nozzles last a long time, even when they are constructed entirely from materials such as stainless steel or aluminum. However, they still benefit from superior air/media accelerating designs. Ergonomic and durability considerations are evident in Clemco nozzle designs. Most Clemco nozzle lines feature durable and easy-to-hold surfaces made from rubber and other resilient materials.

Clemco manufactures a full line of hose and hose-connecting accessories and supplies. Cabinet systems are typically operated by foot pedals

This Clemco Nozzle-Remote 2 remotely controls the pressure pot connected to it. It shuts the system down when the handle is released, acting as a control and as a deadman safety device. This unit is pneumatically operated. Optional electrical controls can also be fitted to it.

that employ either pneumatic or electric signals to operate the blast pot or siphon system valves. Pneumatic controls are still the most common, but electric controls are gaining on them. Clemco sells a full line of both types.

If you drop a blast nozzle hose assembly in a cabinet, not much that is bad happens because you almost automatically come off your foot switch to shut down the blast. However, if you drop a nozzle and handle assembly in a blast room or outside blasting situation, there is real, even great, danger, depending on the air volume and pressure of the system.

For booth and outside blasting situations, deadman hand valves are a necessary precaution. The deadman valve is simply a valve that an operator must make a conscious effort to keep open. The deadman control idea originated in railroad and street-car practice in the 19th Century. If an operator lost consciousness, or was otherwise incapacitated, the control was automatically released and the operation that it controlled was shut down.

Deadman blasting valves require that a hand lever be squeezed by an operator to commence and to continue blasting. These valves are typically connected to remote blast control valves by air pressure that signals operation to commence or cease at a pressure pot. They also stop operation if the pressure line connecting them to pressure pot valving is severed. These valves are sometimes called "remote valves," because they control blast operation from a distance. Inexpensive mechanical deadman valves are often available for less expensive consumer equipment. The remotely controlled valves manufactured by high-end companies, such as Clemco, are much safer and more convenient than the mechanical style.

In contrast to the need for deadman valves in booth and outside blasting, in-cabinet blasting almost never requires any kind of safety system for the air that the blast system operator breathes. Because the operator should be all but completely separated from the blast air, it presents little or no hazard to his or her health. However, in blast booth and outdoor blasting situations, the blast operator and others near the blast area breathe the contaminated blast air if they are not protected from it. It is almost needless to say, but

If you do much blasting with silica sand, you need a respirator hood and silica-free air to supply it. This 3/4–hp Clemco Calipso oil-free pump will supply air that is safe to breathe via durable light gauge hoses when the pump unit is placed outside of the blast area.

exhausting dangerous cabinet blast air into space occupied by human beings is something that should never be allowed or done.

In situations where operators, and/or others, are in areas where they would be likely to breathe dangerous blast air, provision must be made for them to breathe clean air supplied from outside the blast area. In some cases, highly filtered or bottled air is also acceptable and practical, depending on the type of contamination involved. The most obvious contaminant is silica from blasting with silica sand. I have already discussed the disease silicosis (see Chapter 6).

In blasting situations where silicosis or other breathing hazards exist, the operator's breathing air must be supplied either from tanks of compressed breathing air, or by pumps that draw their air from outside the blast area and/or filter it.

One obvious idea is to breathe air supplied by the compressor that supplies the blast air. This would be convenient. It would also be *deadly*. Breathing the oils and carbons in air supplied by large compressors, either piston or screw type, on anything like a regular or prolonged basis leads to severe illness, and possibly death. Lesser exposures may seem to have less serious consequences but are still too dangerous to be acceptable.

The two safe, approved sources of breathing air for the sandblasting hoods that operators wear are properly prepared cylinders of air designed expressly for human consumption, or from oil-less, diaphragm-type compressors that are specially designed to pump breathing air. These air supplies carry various names. My favorite is "mine air safety." Manufacturers, such as Clemco, always certify them

to supply human breathing air. *Never* attempt to supply a blast hood with air from your shop compressor.

Blasting on a Budget

A dedicated hobbyist can blast his or her way from a grungy, corroded frame to a pristine frame. It can be done with an inexpensive blast outfit, plus a good 5-hp compressor and about $70 worth of quartz sand. Interested? Read on.

In Chapter 5 I followed Frank Weinert as he blast stripped the cab of a large old truck. It was a professional job, done expertly, thoroughly, and quickly. In the back of my mind, I considered how the work of an amateur, employing very minimal and inexpensive equipment, would compare to Frank's results. Could an amateur reach Frank's level of quality? How long would it take to complete a medium to large proj-

ect if the person doing the blasting lacked Frank's experience? Would it even be worth attempting a medium to large job without the things that Frank had?

At about the same time as I was pondering these questions, my friend Rob turned up with a blasting project that offered some possibilities for making the comparison. He needed to strip an early 1960s Triumph TR-3 frame for the eventual mounting of a Devin fiberglass body.

Although blasting the frame of a small sports car does not present the degree of difficulty or square surface area that Frank's truck cab project did, it still represents a medium-size blasting job, mainly due to the intricacies of the frame. However, unlike Frank's project, the Triumph frame had no delicate sheet metal that could be easily warped by blasting. Therefore, while Rob's frame project required considerable patience,

Steam cleaning revealed the almost naked truth of Rob's TR-3 frame, and it was good. The metal surfaces, welds, and rivets all looked sound. The final truth would arrive after Rob sandblasted his frame.

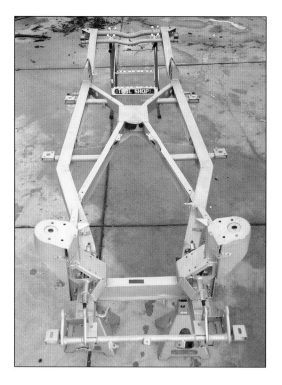

Here is what Rob saw when all paint and rust had been blasted off his frame. Blasting left an ideal surface for coating adhesion. With proper application, the finish on this frame will look great for decades because it is built up on a sound base.

Rob's blast rig is on the cheap, but there's nothing wrong with that. It's great for occasional blasting; inexpensive, durable enough, and convenient. It holds two bags of sand, good for a half hour of blasting, and has a reliable deadman valve. The only upgrade is an improved moisture trap.

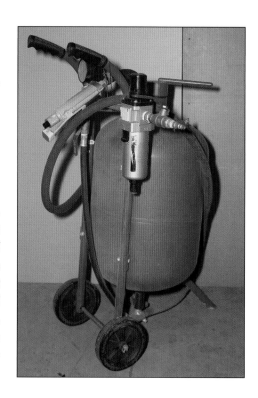

Before you start any blasting job, it's important to assess just what you are getting into. Look for features, such as delicate surfaces, that might warp or cut through under blasting. This job looks remarkably free of any lurking problems.

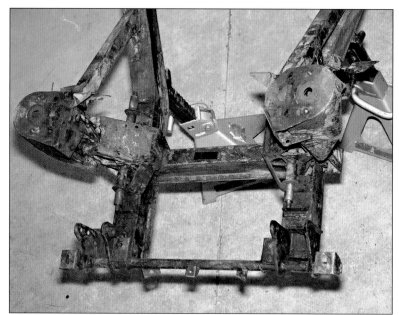

Always inspect jobs from as many angles as possible when you plan your blasting attacks. Tar undercoating that is not visible in this photograph becomes quite obvious in the next one. This should be removed with solvent and a scraper before blasting continues; otherwise, blasting may spread it around.

Note the threads on the forward facing shock absorber mounts and spring perch tops. They can survive light blasting. However, the area under the tape on top of the box crossmember has a delicate nameplate that has been protected with resilient tape.

Frank is an extremely experienced and skilled blast operator. Rob is relatively new to this work. Enormous advantage Frank.

Frank's equipment cost thousands of dollars.

Rob's equipment cost was barely into the hundreds of dollars. Advantage? Well, that depends on your point of view and how much you value your time.

Both Frank and Rob used about the same amount of sand to do their respective jobs, around 500 pounds. But Frank's job involved much more surface area. In material and time use efficiency, it was clearly, advantage Frank.

Frank's results were as close to perfect as any abrasive blasting results that I have ever seen.

Rob's results were also about as good as any that abrasive blasting could yield, although on a less challenging project. A draw.

My conclusion is that if a blasting job is relatively simple and has no complex issues, such as warping or blasting through thin and/or delicate sections of sheet metal, a modestly equipped amateur can achieve excellent results, albeit using a lot of abrasive media and a lot of time. Along that route, he or she can save some money and take great pride in his or her accomplishment. That last point offers considerable value, too.

it did not call for the fine judgment on which Frank's truck cab had depended to avoid warping its large sheet-metal panels.

Although Frank's work was completed in a few hours, using soda and quartz sandblasting approaches, Rob's much smaller quartz sandblasting job consumed about 9 hours of blasting time in two separate sessions.

For the purposes of comparison, Frank's air supply was a diesel-driven rotary screw compressor, delivering air at a rate of 385 cfm. Frank's air was dried in a condensing refrigeration unit.

Rob used a 5-hp 20-cfm compressor with a simple bowl-type drier. Advantage Frank.

Frank was blasting at 90 psi through a nitrided 1/2-inch nozzle.

Rob was also blasting at 90 psi, but through a 3/16-inch ceramic nozzle. Advantage Frank.

Rob's Progress Step by Step

Rob's TR-3 frame was very rusty, with deep, pitting rust in some areas. A potpourri of old paint, solidified grease, oil, road tar, and other assorted grunge covered most of its surface. A small amount of surface still bore factory paint.

Rob's first step was to use an atomizing siphon sprayer to pre-soak the frame in an S-C Degreaser and kerosene mix, a commercial solvent designed to soften grunge for steam cleaning. After half an hour of pre-soaking, Rob steam cleaned his frame. The result was an undramatic but critical change in the frame's surface. It could now be blasted without spreading grease around and pounding it into the pores of the metal.

The next step was to sandblast the frame. For this job, Rob used a light-duty 110-pound blast pot that came in a kit with a nozzle, operator hood, media funnel, blast nozzle

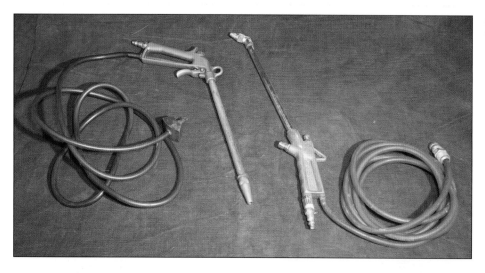

1 *The siphon spray device on the left was used to pre-soak the frame in an atomized mixture of S-C Degreaser and kerosene. That softened up the grunge on the frame and made steam cleaning it easier and more effective.*

2 *Rob began blasting, concentrating on the large surface areas and trying to get a lot of surface cleaned quickly. Later, he went over the frame again to begin working on its intricacies and details.*

3 *Because the TR-3 frame is light and easy to handle, Rob blasted the top horizontal and side vertical surfaces on its top and bottom sides separately. There is never a need to crawl under anything that can be turned over manually or rotated.*

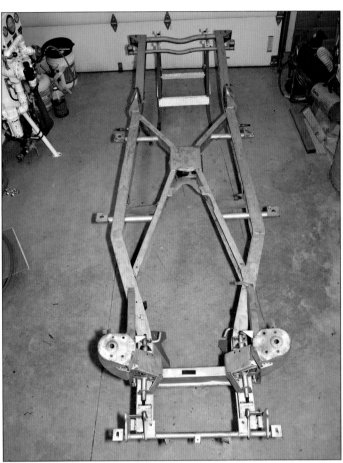

4 In this and the previous photograph, you can see Rob blasting up, and then down, in the same area. Normally he wouldn't do this, but he was obsessed with removing a rust spot. At this point, the frame is cleaner than it was, but still far from spotless.

5 This is what the frame looked like when Rob began his second blasting session. Note that it looks much cleaner in direct sunlight.

6 After the first blasting session, the frame was stored in a dry, heated building until weather provided the opportunity to finish blasting it. The second session included the advantage of bright sunlight.

7 Rob's second blasting session involved going over all of the frame's surfaces two more times. Each pass yielded a better result, because Rob kept discovering areas that he had missed, or failed to clean completely.

deadman handle valve unit, and four extra ceramic nozzles. The kit cost a bit more than $100. This is really minimalist equipment.

Rob discarded the low-quality air pressure regulator and air drier unit that came with the kit and substituted a higher-quality version. Beyond that, the pressure pot and accessories that came with it were stock.

One advantage of using a small blast pot and nozzle and limited air supply is that Rob moved very slowly across the surfaces that he was blasting. This gave him lots of time to observe those surfaces as he blasted them. They were not buried under a fog of blast media.

After blasting for four and a half hours, Rob was tired, but the frame was pretty clean. It was free of most heavy and deep, pitted rust, but there was still work to do to finish removing all visible rust. At this point, Rob's first blast session was ended only because of impending darkness. The frame was stored inside in a dry, heated building to await the next blasting opportunity.

It was about a week before a day that was warm and dry enough

8 *Minor rusting had occurred in some places during the week between blasting sessions. This, too, had to be removed.*

9 *As Rob blasted, the frame got cleaner and cleaner, and Rob got fussier and fussier. When things are going well, it's sometimes hard to know when to quit. Factors such as rain or darkness usually aid in making these decisions.*

10 *Even a bare frame presents visibility problems in some areas, and you end up blasting blind. In this case, turning the frame over or working from its other side usually opened every area to clear viewing. This viewing redundancy is very useful.*

11 *The in-facing inside outside surface of this bracket is an example of an area that is only really visible from the other side of the frame. Good blasting practice identifies such areas and accounts for them.*

12 *Rob spent a lot of time on this bracket and succeeded in blasting it completely clean. A good statement of Murphy's Law, as it applies to abrasive blasting, is "nature always sides with the hidden defect." That defect, if not corrected, is always where problems begin.*

13 Note the very different blast distances from nozzle to target that Rob employs in blasting this frame. This is a trade-off situation. Blasting from a greater distance covers a wider area, but you have to move more slowly.

14 The finished frame looks great. It was oriented in many positions and blown off with dry compressed air to remove all sand. Now, speed was essential to protect it from airborne humidity. Even on a dry day, visible flash rusting can occur within a few hours.

15 Within 15 minutes of finishing his blasting work, Rob sprayed the frame with Ospho phosphatizing and etching solution. The excess Ospho was then hosed off and the frame was allowed to air dry.

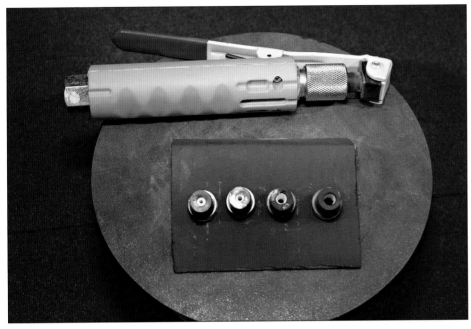

16 *Nozzles are a key blasting component. Inexpensive nozzles, such as those shown here, are not very durable. Their output ends, shown after 30, 60, 90, and 120 minutes of use (left to right), make this point. As the nozzle apertures become larger, their effectiveness and efficiency decreases, proportionally. As you can see, these nozzles are good for about an hour, maybe an hour and a half, of use at the 90-psi blasting pressure with quartz sand.*

17 *Examined at their input ends, the smooth flow and venturi-effect acceleration design of these primitive ceramic nozzles progressively disappears. These features are missing entirely from the two-hour-use nozzle (far right).*

for Rob to finish blasting his frame arrived. By then, some light surface rust was on some of the areas that he had blasted in his first session, and some areas where he had not reached bare metal, but the worst of the heavy rust was pretty much removed.

Rob started his second blasting session early on a late fall day, when outdoor blasting was unlikely, but still possible. Although the blasting process works perfectly well at low temperatures, the human doing the blasting tends to suffer in those conditions.

In his second blasting session, Rob took the frame to clean white metal.

It is never possible to state accurately that "all corrosion, paint, and other contaminants were removed from the surface," but Rob came as close to that standard as is humanly possible. The frame was turned over and put on its sides and bottom several times to give Rob access to all of its outer surfaces. It would be difficult, if not impossible, to do a more thorough job. The session lasted between four and five hours.

When blasting was completed, Rob and I blew the frame off, with particular attention to blowing out its boxed side sections. Then, we oriented it in as many positions as possible and rocked and shook the sand out of its intricacies. During this operation we used soothing language to help persuade the sand out of the frame's inner intricacies. This *may* have helped. After that, we did some more blowing and some more shaking until we could no longer dislodge any sand from the frame.

The next step was to immediately protect the frame from corrosion that might be caused by airborne moisture and/or handling. We used an atomizing sprayer to cover it with Ospho (a phosphatizing, anti-rust product). Ospho is an old metal prep product (technically, a "conversion coating") that protects metal from rust and enhances paint adhesion.

Blast nozzle life is an interesting issue. High-quality, professional nozzles last for hundreds of hours or longer, depending on their construction and the media used in them. However, the nozzles that Rob used for his TR-3 frame project did not last long. He went through six new nozzles in the course of working on his TR-3 project.

Consumer-Grade Blasting Equipment

All photos in this section are courtesy of The Eastwood Company.

The Eastwood Company is among the oldest, and is certainly the largest, of companies dedicated exclusively to purveying equipment, tools, and supplies to the automotive hobbies. This includes, most notably, restoration, customizing, fabrication, hot rodding, and home auto repair. On the way to assuming that position, a funny thing happened to Eastwood products. Professional refinishers, body men, mechanics, and assorted other professionals began to take serious notice of those Eastwood products.

Today, it is common to see Eastwood equipment, tools, and supplies in professional settings, including some of the premier shops in the country. This is, of course, a great compliment to the Eastwood Company's reputation for quality, innovation, and customer support, among other positive attributes.

Although the Eastwood Company remains focused on the consumer end of automotive endeavors, some of its products have, by now, found comfortable places in the professional and commercial realms.

Presently, the Eastwood Company offers four different abrasive blasting cabinets in its catalog. The most basic is PN 20027, available for around $400. This is a great starter cabinet for someone who wants to get into abrasive blasting with a small, but

The Eastwood PN 30721 table-top blast cabinet system is an affordable and well thought-out unit for small- to medium-size parts. Powder coated for durability, this cabinet comes with inside lighting, a siphon-type gun, an abrasive pickup, gloves, and window protectors.

Eastwood's basic blast cabinet, the PN 20027, offers a 33-inch-wide by 24-inch-deep blast platform and can enclose objects up to almost 2 feet tall. It comes with a suction-type gun and pickup and replaceable ceramic nozzle. Gloves are also included, as is a fluorescent lighting system.

The PN 20027 Eastwood cabinet's wide opening top door allows easy loading and avoids the media spillage that can occur with side entry doors. Removable lens protectors reduce the need to replace the viewing glass. A hinged bottom port makes it easy to change media, while an available dust collector completes the system.

versatile, unit. It ships as parts. According to Eastwood literature, two people can assemble it in about two hours. Its basic configuration is well designed for easy loading through a hinged top window panel. Media removal is also easy to accomplish via its hinged and latched bottom port. This cabinet ships with a siphon blast gun and gauntlet gloves. It features an easily replaceable window and comes with window liners that prolong window life.

Although this unit uses a manually loaded and operated siphon system, not a fully automated pressure pot–type system, it can be adapted to pressure pot operation. It costs a fraction of an automated pressure pot system with integrated cabinet. It is also much simpler to maintain, while still fulfilling the essential needs of most hobbyists and of many small shops to blast small- to medium-size parts on an occasional basis.

Eastwood offers an inexpensive dust collector kit for its basic blast cabinet. This is a universal dust collector setup that can be mounted on any small- to medium-size cabinet. And produces enough air movement volume to keep such a cabinet clear of media and debris. This is important, because without an air stream of sufficient volume and velocity to clear a cabinet, it becomes impossible to view what is being blasted with sufficient clarity to blast effectively. A dust collector or reclaim unit also allows recycling of any reclaimable media that you blast.

Eastwood offers two cabinets larger than PN 20027 and one that is smaller, PN 30721. The latter is an intriguing bench-top cabinet that sells for about $150. That price includes a siphon gun and media pickup, internal fluorescent lighting, and gauntlet gloves. A medium-size shop vacuum keeps the cabinet's 3-cubic-foot blast area clear. This system's gun has a 10 cfm air requirement.

Small to medium objects are loaded through this cabinet's hinged top door and can be viewed easily through the cabinet's 19 x 15–inch top window. Cabinet platform dimensions are about 1.5 x 2 feet. Its window features tear-away lens protectors for prolonged window life.

For both in-cabinet and outside blasting, Eastwood offers two different suction gun systems. One features steel nozzles and the other uses

The PN 20027 doesn't exactly "swallow" this header "with room to spare," but it does provide enough room to blast it. The header must be turned and reoriented a few times to gain blast access to all of its surfaces.

The hinged and clasped hopper output on the bottom of Eastwood's PN 20027 cabinet provides an easy way to remove its media content. This feature comes in handy when you want to change media type, or if you convert it to pressure pot operation and need to change the pressure pot locations.

The Eastwood PN 30998 dust collector kit comes with everything that you need to mount it on and connect it to an existing blast cabinet. It features a 12-amp motor and replaceable filter, clears dust from a medium-size cabinet, and can hold 1.75 gallons of cleaned media for reuse.

Eastwood offers various inexpensive siphon-type blast guns fitted with easily replaceable ceramic nozzles. This one is typical of these designs. Siphon blast guns have the virtue of simplicity but lack the efficiency of the pressure-type guns that are used with much more expensive pressure pot systems.

Eastwood's entry-level cabinet, the PN 30721, is a great way to get into abrasive blasting. It's inexpensive and comes with everything that you need to blast, except, of course, a compressor. Later, if you buy a larger cabinet, you probably will keep this one around for its benchtop convenience.

Shown here is the back of an Eastwood PN 20027 blast cabinet with a PN 30998 dust collector mounted on it. A baffled connection between the two units, roughly at the middle of the dust collector, extracts air from the cabinet. Recycled media is removed from the bottom of the dust collector.

Here is another Eastwood siphon-type gun design. It is shown here in kit form with three replaceable steel nozzles and a changeable air orifice below them. Note the material pickup to the right of the gun and the hose.

ceramic nozzles. These guns are easily plumbed to a pickup container, or directly into the cabinet's bottom hopper, and have the virtues of being simple and easy to maintain. Replacement nozzles are inexpensive and can be changed quickly and easily.

Despite those virtues, siphon guns lack efficiency; they require a great deal more air to operate than comparable pressure pot and gun setups. That factor can approach a five-to-one disadvantage for siphon-type guns. In other words,

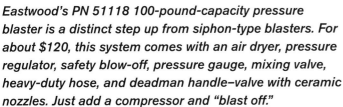

Eastwood's PN 51118 100-pound-capacity pressure blaster is a distinct step up from siphon-type blasters. For about $120, this system comes with an air dryer, pressure regulator, safety blow-off, pressure gauge, mixing valve, heavy-duty hose, and deadman handle–valve with ceramic nozzles. Just add a compressor and "blast off."

Three valves control the PN 51118 blast system. The valve on the top right controls the compressed air entering the system. The valve to its left, just below it, controls the blast stream. The valve under the pot (barely visible in this photograph) controls the critical media-to-air blast mixture ratio.

as much as 80 percent of the air that you consume with a siphon gun system is simply lifting the media from below and into your gun, and nothing more. What's left over propels the media toward its target. Pressure guns use about 90 percent of the air that goes through them to propel media. That's a big difference.

Eastwood's cabinets are easily converted from siphon gun to pressure gun operation, and because siphon guns are inexpensive, the conversion really doesn't waste much money should you choose to make it. This means that as your resources permit, you can always upgrade to pressure pot operation without having to scrap a whole system. If you have added a reclaim unit to a siphon gun system, you can continue to use it after you convert to a pressure system.

Eastwood pressure blast pots are also ready to use in blast booths and for outside blasting. This kind of versatility is one of the factors that have made Eastwood blasting equipment widely popular.

Eastwood sells pressure pots in two styles (light-duty screw-plug top and heavy-duty hopper top) in varying media capacities that include 50, 90, 100, 110, 150, 200, and 300 pounds. Each of the two styles comes in some, but not all, of those capacities. Prices vary from a tad more than $100 to about $200 for the screw-plug top pots. The heavier-duty hopper top line runs from around $700 to about $1,100. The latter is the heavy-duty hopper top in its largest, 300-pound-capacity size.

All Eastwood pressure pots come ready to use, complete with a heavy blast hose, a deadman valve, a pressure regulator, a pressure relief valve, a mixing valve, a shutoff valve, a

This Eastwood mechanical deadman valve works with any pressure blaster. The basic valve costs less than $15 from Eastwood. Rubberized ceramic nozzles and other wear parts are also available quite inexpensively. More sophisticated remote control deadman valves can cost a lot more than an entire Eastwood pressure-blasting outfit.

These rubber-clad blast nozzles for Eastwood's deadman valves are inexpensive, but perishable. An hour or two of service is the most you can expect to get from one of them. Some suppliers sell these valves in various orifice sizes for different-capacity air supplies.

pressure gauge, and an air dryer. They can be run on as little as 10 cfm of air, although about twice that amount makes for better and more consistent operation.

The Eastwood deadman valve and pot may seem familiar because they are similar to the equipment that Rob used to sandblast his TR-3 frame. The equipment that he used happened to be from a different supplier, not Eastwood. Regardless, the

Eastwood's mid-range PN 50096 soda blaster ($720) is shipped with conversion plumbing that equips it for non-soda-media blasting, as desired. The changeover is claimed to be fast and easy. As a soda blaster, this 100-pound-capacity unit features a heavy-duty deadman valve and many other features and attributes.

This is the heart of Eastwood's consumer soda-blasting outfits. It's available separately for under $90, to convert almost any non-soda-blast pot to soda operation. Converting an existing pot that you own to soda can be a good way to experience soda blasting to see if you like it.

equipment from Eastwood is inexpensive for what you get and quite useful for many blasting projects, even fairly large ones. The Eastwood pots have a full complement of function, safety, and convenience features. They are easy to refill, operate, and adjust.

Eastwood's basic deadman valve/nozzle costs about $15, with replacement nozzles for it going for about $3 each. Other wear parts for these

units are also available from Eastwood, very inexpensively.

For basic soda blasting, Eastwood sells two different pressure pots. Both have 100-pound capacity. The lighter-duty pot is based on its 100-pound abrasive blasting pot for non-soda applications. Outfitted with Eastwood's soda conversion plumbing and a deadman handle with a ceramic nozzle, it sells for about $250. A much-heavier-duty

100-pound soda pressure pot with a hopper top and generally heavier construction sells for around $700 with similar accessories.

It should be noted that Eastwood sells universal soda-blasting retro fit kits for both siphon and pressure pot systems. The kit for pressure systems is less than $70. These conversion kits, and the blasters based on them, do not produce the top-line efficiency of commercial soda-blasting systems, but they are useful for occasional soda-blasting jobs and cost thousands less than the more efficient commercial systems. Put another way, if you need to blast an occasional carburetor, alloy cylinder head, or transmission case, the Eastwood systems will do just fine by you.

Eastwood also offers a commercial grade soda-blasting system with a 100-pound-capacity pot and many advanced control and metering features. At around $2,000, this system is probably beyond the needs

The idea here is simple; two pots for two blast media choices. You can blast with soda or another medium of your choice, or you can mix them in any proportion. Making your selection is simple. It's done with the red and green valves, just behind the deadman control handle.

These red- and green-handled metering/on-off valves control the flow of each of the two types of media in Eastwood's Dual Blast system. You can make running adjustments as you blast. This is much less cumbersome than hauling two completely separate blast systems to your blast site, and managing them.

Working on automobiles usually involves dealing with many different materials in differing conditions. The array of parts behind the Eastwood Master Blaster-Dual Blaster amply illustrates this point. Using soda and a more aggressive media, separately, or combined in varying proportions, is a great way to deal with these differences.

and/or resources of most hobbyists. Still, you can dream.

Finally, in the blaster category, Eastwood offers an intriguing double blast pressure pot system called the "Eastwood Master Blaster-Dual Blaster" for about $350, fully equipped. This system has two separate pressure pots, one set up for soda blasting and the other capable of using almost any other blast media. A mixing valve just behind the blast valve/nozzle handle allows the use of either or both pots singly, or in any proportion. You can blast straight soda, or you can blast straight sand, garnet, aluminum oxide, etc. Or, by adjusting two valves that are located conveniently behind the blast handle, you can blast any mixture of soda and another abrasive.

This system is particularly useful when you are blasting a variety of different parts made from differ-

ent metals or in different formats, or other materials. It is also convenient for blasting single assemblies that contain different materials, or materials in different formats. In these cases, where changing the media from a non-aggressive to an aggressive blast, or vice versa, improves your blasting results, the Eastwood Dual Blaster is a great solution.

Air filtration and regulation are important for great media blasting. Eastwood's PN 20472 Filter Separator Regulator combination unit employs two-stage coalescing filtration for your compressed air. It removes particles and moisture in stage one, and oil and other aerosols in stage two. An air pressure regulator completes this $250 unit.

Essentially, it replaces two separate pots with two separate plumbing systems with one integrated two-pot system.

Consumer-Grade Blasting Supplies and Accessories

Eastwood sells many abrasive blasting accessory and supply

Eastwood's PN 20473 2-Stage Air Drying system employs a first-stage coalescing oil and aerosol filtration unit. Its second stage is a desiccant dryer that requires some routine maintenance to keep it running dry. At slightly over $275, this unit can serve as a small shop's air filtration and drying system.

Eastwood's sturdy hardware basket for abrasive blasting offers a great convenience for blasting small parts. This is a great alternative to chasing the lost parts that escape your grip through your blast system. This basket retains your parts and makes viewing as you blast easy.

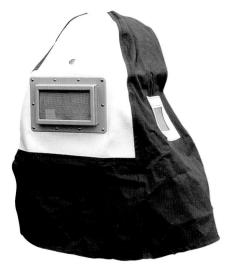

In the realm of important blasting accessories, a stalwart blast hood is paramount. Eastwood's vented $40 Deluxe Abrasive Blasting Hood fits that bill. Its sound design, good materials, and quality construction make it a great choice for both outdoor and booth blasting.

products. Some items are intended for maintaining or upgrading existing Eastwood equipment but are not limited to that purpose. Many of them can be used for maintaining or upgrading non-Eastwood equipment, and even as basic parts for custom building your own equipment or system. Some Eastwood blast support products are just plain handy aids to blasting.

Moisture separators perfectly exemplify this Eastwood product category. Eastwood pressure pots are shipped with moisture separators as part of the package. You can also buy Eastwood moisture separators to replace worn units or to upgrade to more effective driers. These products vary from vortex-type coalescing units that trap particles, oil, and moisture to more advanced desiccant-type separators. The latter contain desiccant beads that absorb moisture from the air passing through them. When the beads are saturated with moisture, they can be removed from the drier and baked dry for reuse, or they can be replaced with new, dry beads.

In the industrial world, beyond coalescing and desiccant driers, there are deliquescent- and refrigeration-type moisture separators, but those run into hundreds or thousands of dollars. What Eastwood offers is more than adequate for most small-scale abrasive blasting purposes.

Eastwood offers a high-quality vented blasting hood for blasting booth and outside use. It features a generously sized acrylic lens and adjustable helmet support straps for better positioning and comfort. Its gray, brown, and white plastic, sim

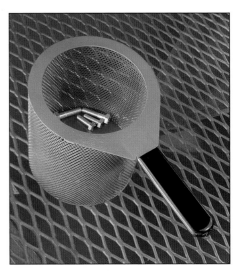

Many, even most, parts lost in blasting are recovered. The issue is the time and frustration that finding them requires. The bolts nestled in this basket look placid in this photograph. But, in the fog of blasting, hanging on to them individually can be challenging.

ulated leather, and fabric surfaces protect your head and shoulders from abrasive blast. It can also make a definite fashion statement. In combination with other garments, this blasting hood has great potential on the Halloween circuit.

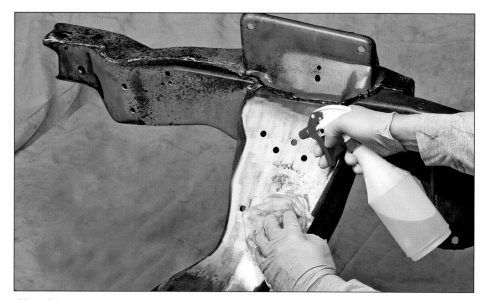

After Blast can be applied with a plastic spray bottle. It should be allowed to sit for a short time and then wiped off. How long its protection from rust will last depends on temperature, humidity, and other factors.

Eastwood's After Blast, as its name suggests, is designed to treat freshly blasted items. It cleans and etches steel, cast iron, and aluminum surfaces, removing blast dust while lightly etching them for improved paint adhesion. It also bonds zinc phosphate to blasted parts for long-term anti-rust protection.

In the area of "perishables and consumables," that is, supplies that you will certainly need for replacing worn blasting system–related parts, Eastwood offers quality products such as blast hose, control valves, nozzles, cabinet gauntlet gloves, and more.

The Eastwood blasting accessory that I find particularly useful is its hardware basket for abrasive blasting. This sturdily constructed metal basket contains small parts for blasting in your blast cabinet or outside it. You can shake the parts around in the basket to rearrange them to expose their different surfaces.

If you have ever tried to hold a small part, such as a nut or screw, in a thickly gloved hand while you blast it, you will appreciate the convenience of being able to blast many small parts in a basket at the same time. Few things are as frustrating as trying to hold several small parts, one after another, while you blast them. Another exasperating act is having to dig into and sift the blasting media in your cabinet hopper and/or reclaim unit to retrieve lost small part(s).

Eastwood's "After Blast" is an etching product that is similar to the Ospho product I referred to previously. It is basically a phosphatizing metal prep that cleans and etches to protect clean metal and to prepare it for coating. After Blast also adds a zinc phosphate coating to that protection.

Freshly blasted metal is extremely vulnerable to flash rusting. On a humid day in warm weather, you can sometimes see metal flash rusting within minutes of being blasted. However, if you use a good metal prep, such as After Blast, you can stop that rusting for days or weeks. That's plenty of time to cover it with a coating that permanently protects blasted metal from moisture.

As with any good metal prep, After Blast also etches clean metal and provides a near ideal surface for primer, paint, or other coating adhesion. I consider the use of a good product in this class to be essential to sound abrasive blasting practice.

Sources

For many of the metal cleaning methods described in this book you will find the necessary equipment and supplies in the usual places: hardware stores, farm stores, lumber yards, auto body shop supply stores, catalog mail order establishments, and online vendors. Finding sandpaper, scrapers, parts solvent, abrasive discs, steam cleaning detergent, etc., is not challenging. Some sources of these items may be less expensive than others, and others may reliably sell higher quality merchandise than their competitors. Your own experiences and those of friends and acquaintances will quickly lead you to the best sources for hand tools, power tools, abrasive papers, wire brushes, and the like, as well as the best prices for them.

Much of this book is devoted to abrasive media blasting. Suppliers of equipment for abrasive blasting processes are more limited and more difficult to find than for simple hardware, tools, and supplies. The following suggestions may help you in these quests.

Blasting equipment such as cabinets, pressure pots, and dust collectors falls into two categories, industrial and consumer. Two major suppliers are featured in Chapter 7, one in each of these categories. In the case of consumer equipment and supplies, I chose to highlight the offerings of the Eastwood Company because it has the most complete lines of consumer blasting supplies and equipment, from bagged or drummed abrasives to blast nozzles,

gloves, cabinets, siphon systems, and pressure pots. Eastwood's range of products begins well above the cheap junk tier and goes through consumer equipment and on up to light industrial equipment.

Its products have proven to be of good quality, value, and durability. They are available via the Eastwood Company catalog, online mail order, and through an increasing number of Eastwood retail stores. At the top of the range of products offered by the Eastwood Company you can even find some commercial grade equipment.

Other mass retailers that sell somewhat comparable, but less complete, lines of blasting equipment to the public are the Northern Tool and Equipment Company and the Harbor Freight and Salvage Company. Like the Eastwood Company, these retailers sell through printed catalogs, online, and through retail stores. The main difference between Eastwood and these other two companies is that Eastwood's products

are aimed exclusively at automotive endeavors while the others are more generally purposed.

Harbor Freight is, for example, one of the largest customers (maybe *the* largest) for ARMEX baking soda in the United States. ARMEX baking soda is the bestselling brand of bicarbonate of soda in the United States, and probably the world. If the name *ARMEX* is not familiar to you, think of Arm & Hammer, it's the same outfit.

For a 50-pound bag of Armex Maintenance Formula XL (extra-large particle, and the most generally useful grade of ARMEX soda) Harbor Freight charges around $40 in-store, and adds a flat rate of about $7 for ground shipping to your door. Eastwood's price for the same product is similar.

There are certainly cheaper ways to buy soda. If you order blasting grade soda by pallets of 50-pound bags, it costs less per bag, and a dozen pallets cost still less than one pallet. If you buy it in bulk, by the ton, it

I purchased this vintage Zero/Clemco blast cabinet and dust collector/pressure pot used unit from a company in Milwaukee 35 years ago. It has served admirably since. Any parts that I needed for it I could either make or buy. It cost me $250, a great value.

is still cheaper. However, if you are doing occasional soda blasting, Harbor Freight and the Eastwood Company are among the best deals that you are likely to find for the soda that you need.

What holds true for soda is also true of other blast abrasives, such as aluminum oxide, glass bead, garnet, and plastic media. In these cases, Eastwood is likely to be your best bet for small quantities. For blasting sand you should check out local sources such as lumberyards and home supply stores. Some of these stores may sell other blasting media, such as copper slag.

The other major source for blasting equipment and supplies is regional distributors. You can find these companies in your local Yellow Pages under headings such as "Abrasive Blasting Equipment" and "Abrasive Blasting Suppliers." Sometimes you find them under headings beginning with the word "Sandblasting." You can also find this type of vendor with an Internet search. Most suppliers in this class are located in or near large metropolitan areas.

Here's a word of advice for dealing with regional distributors of blasting equipment and materials. If you operate a small commercial shop, they may be somewhat happy to see you and to do business with you. It is unlikely that they will be overjoyed. These businesses tend to generate the greatest portion of their revenue by selling expensive equipment and frequently repeated large orders for abrasive cleaning supplies. With some few exceptions, if you show up with a pickup truck or minivan wanting three or five bags of aluminum oxide, pulverized walnut shells, or glass bead, do not expect to make their day. They are geared to fairly high volume and value sales as well as frequent purchases by their customers.

You can probably persuade a regional distributor to sell you small quantities of blasting media, but don't expect an industrial quantity price for what you purchase. The

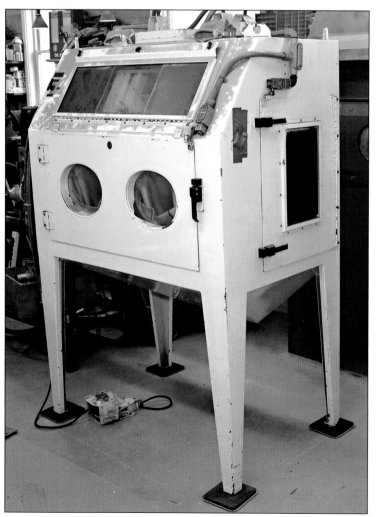

This Ruemelin soda-blast cabinet joined my blasting equipment recently. It's close to 25 years old and shows absolutely no wear. After a cleanup it will look almost new. You cannot buy consumer equipment that matches it in quality or utility.

This is a newer Ruemelin soda-blast cabinet that recently joined our equipment profile. It takes some hunting to find equipment such as this, but it is more often than not worth the effort.

This Mott cabinet is older than I am, by several years. Built out of 1/8-inch-thick plate, it's rugged beyond necessity. It's also fairly awkward to use. Over the years I retrofitted it with several conveniences and improvement features to civilize it. I think I paid $150 for it.

This 1960s Ruemelin 6-foot round cabinet's counter-weighted top raises and swings aside to admit large objects. Its turntable rotates to position them. For blasting large items in a cabinet, there's nothing like it. I bought it for $175 about 30 years ago, including more than 500 pounds of 220-grit silicon carbide that was inside it.

An oddity, this stainless wet blaster (liquid hone) came to me on the cheap. I never found much use for its great theoretical capabilities. Now it languishes in storage. As they say, "It seemed like a good idea at the time." As they also say, "You can't win 'em all."

A fully instrumented Schmidt blasting pot is a treasure for soda-blasting work. I was tipped off to this one, used and in very good condition. It and the Ruemelin cabinet are the basis for our small soda-blasting operation.

Many years ago I needed a very small cabinet to walnut shell–blast some parts. Using an old industrial canister, I created this cabinet in a day. It had lighting, a fixed or mobile nozzle, and a siphon blast system. It worked pretty well, too.

On a whim, I purchased this stainless industrial hopper. I'm not sure why. My latest idea for using it is to build a stand to plop it onto, fabricate a hinged lid with a window and lighting, and use it as a final blow-off station for blasted parts. It may yet happen.

Used industrial equipment exists all over the place. All you have to do is find it. It may well be worth the effort; I have often found used industrial blast cabinets and pressure pots at prices that are excitingly low. I have seen this equipment at swap meets, at industrial equipment dealers, and advertised in various listings of used equipment in print and on the Internet.

Often, used industrial blasting equipment has features and capabilities that you will never need. Wet blasting and material handling modifications to basic blast cabinets and systems come to mind. When you look at equipment loaded with this stuff, you need to calculate whether it is useful to you, or can be easily removed, and whether its existence is reflected in the asking price for the equipment.

Some industrial equipment is pretty bulky and heavy. That can make it difficult to move and to locate on your premises. The upside of used industrial equipment is that it is built to work long hours and for many years. If you choose to go the used industrial route, be sure to educate yourself on what to look for before you examine it, or bring someone along with experience and a cool head as your advisor.

Building your own blast cabinets and other equipment items may be possible, depending on your facilities and capabilities. This is sometimes practical. I wouldn't recommend building a large cabinet yourself, because if you had the capability to do this your time would probably be too valuable to spend on this kind of one-off project. However, building a small cabinet for a specific purpose may make more sense than buying a new or used one. It depends on what you can do and what you want to accomplish.

same goes for parts for commercial blasting units. You may have to search for a supplier to sell you these items new. Don't expect a regional distributor to spend a lot of time educating you about the products that it offers. It is not geared to doing business with the general public. There are exceptions to this, of course, and if you are persistent and/or lucky enough to find one that welcomes small orders, cherish and nurture that contact. In other words, plan on bringing your own coffee.

Ebay and several other auction-type websites offer extensive listings for abrasives, as well as for new and used blasting equipment.

Most interesting to me in buying blast equipment are the two final frontiers: used industrial equipment and home-built equipment.

MY CONCLUSIONS

This book has looked at the general topic of cleaning metal, different kinds of metal, conditions of metal, and approaches to cleaning it. It has considered approaches in terms of what results are appropriate to specific jobs and what level of efficiency is desirable, among other factors.

In general, I have identified three broad classes of metal cleaning methods: chemical and electrochemical, mechanical abrasive, and air-driven and mechanically driven blasting and peening media processes. I have also described some hybrid and exotic cleaning regimens.

My first conclusion is that no single process is the magic bullet for cleaning metal. For example, tumbling or vibrating in various media works well for small fasteners and other small items. However, it is impractical for body panels or rear axle housings. The same is true of cabinet blasting. If you can fit a part into a blast cabinet and orient it favorably for blasting, then blasting it with an appropriate media is often a very fast and thorough way to clean it. So is immersing it in a heated ultrasonic bath, if you have access to that high-investment process.

This fender exhibits a little bit of everything: surface rust, deep rust, primer, and gobbed-on body filler. The only thing missing is paint. Bare metal is the only option here. Considering the alternatives, what do you think is the best cleaning approach?

That is another issue that we have considered, what level of equipment or process is reasonable for a restorer, fabricator, or customizer to own. The answer depends largely on one's means, but certain equipment and processes can be ruled out for ownership purposes without even considering means.

The ultrasonic approach is appropriate to a shop that has the workflow to justify the large investment in an ultrasonic tank and the acquisition of the supplies and knowledge to maintain and use it effectively. However, this item would not make sense for an individual who restores or works on cars at the rate of once or twice a week for three to six hours per session. In his or her case, a blast cabinet system would make much more sense for occasional metal cleaning needs.

Or take the good old electric wire brush wheel. It isn't the best or most efficient way to clean anything. Other approaches are faster, more thorough, less dangerous, and environmentally more sound. Therefore, I should take the five electric wire brush setups in my shop and sell them or send them on to a friend (if I have one) or to charity.

That isn't going to happen, because despite the relative inefficiency and haphazard cleaning done by inexpensive electric wire brush wheels, most of us would be lost without them. Would you really want to clean the plain surfaces and threads of every nut, bolt, screw, bracket, and clamp that you routinely deal with in a blast cabinet, tumble drum, or vibratory device? Probably not. That would be a colossal nuisance.

Sure, I've chased my share of small items around my shop floor and other horizontal surfaces after the little man in the wire brush grabbed them and tossed them somewhere. I've even managed to find *most* of them. It's inconvenient, to say the least. But that's nothing compared to the irritation of having to disassemble the bottom of a blast cabinet to find that kind of item after you have somehow let it slip out

Steam or solvent cleaning is definitely the first step in cleansing this rear end. But what is the next step? Its bulk, weight, and surface complexity preclude approaches such as disc sanding, and it's too big to put in most small chemical tanks. Any ideas?

Ultrasonic cleaning has largely replaced glass bead blasting for cleaning engine parts. It's great if you have the equipment to do it, or even access to that equipment. It represents the high end of chemical cleaning processes. However, tank size precludes it for most cleaning jobs outside of engine parts.

Sandblasting on this scale can be thorough, but slow. Still, if you clean car bodies infrequently, taking a day or two to do it this way might not seem excessive. The cost savings for small equipment over larger equipment is huge, and the results can be just as good.

Behold the lowly wire brush. It is almost never the best way to clean anything, but it is often the most convenient way. In fact, it's so convenient that it is often the first-choice tool for cleaning most small things.

How would you clean this dashboard? Dip-stripping would work but might be pretty inconvenient. Its surface is too complex for any mechanical sanding process. Sandblasting might be too rough, and besides, there is no rust to blast. My vote is for soda blasting. This is the perfect candidate for it.

of your blasting basket or through your gauntlet gloved hands. The good old rotary wire brush produces acceptable results without any fuss or bother, and with minimal effort, and it produces them right now, pronto.

Many cleaning processes have useful places, either in the sense of owning the hardware to perform them, or, in the case of that ultra-sonic tank, having access to a com-mercial unit on a reasonably priced fee basis. Sometimes, even if these processes are not the best or most efficient ones, they are well suited to immediate needs.

Still, for the big jobs there are distinct winners and losers in the competition for the best cleaning methods. Stripping body panels and/or entire cars is one job, in particular, that can be expensive and carries high potential for the several kinds of critical mistakes that can ruin a job. Here, the choices of approach are limited to three: mechanical sanding with a disc sander or other power device; chemical stripping with paint remover or contracting for chemical stripping in a dip tank; and blast cleaning with any one of several media, or combinations of media, with your own equipment or on a service basis.

Cleaning Categories

Considering these three alterna-tives, I have concluded that abrasive blast cleaning is best in most situa-tions and for most end purposes. I believe that its superiority over other methods for a major stripping job extends to several other jobs, such as cleaning automobile frames or large, bulky mechanical components like axle housings and driveshafts. Let's look at the three alternatives.

Category 1

Mechanically applied abrasives, such as disc, DA, jitterbug, and straight-line sanders, are fine for strip-ping paint and rust from panels or off small, relatively flat surfaces, but they are slow. They do not work well on strongly curved surfaces, such as that driveshaft that I mentioned. Of the mechanical sanding approaches, disc sanding is the fastest and most useful approach for larger sanding jobs when you want to go down to bare metal. In fact, it was once the mainstay of stripping body panels and whole bodies.

However, disc sanding requires considerable experience and skill to avoid damaging metal by burning or gouging it. It also can require the removal of a lot of sound metal to

Removing paint and rust mechanically with a disc sander is the traditional way to strip panels. The poly disc, shown here, cuts reasonably quickly and reduces the chances of locally overheating metal. However, it cannot remove deep rust, such as the rust in the photograph under and behind its leading edge.

Disc sanding this mid-1930s door is a practical way to strip it, with some hand sanding on its raised style lines. Its wood framing precludes dip stripping. My choice is to start with soda blasting. That is the least destruc-tive way to discover what lurks beneath the primer.

expunge all of the rust that can live in pits and hollows burrowed into the surfaces of sheet-metal panels. Although disc sanding is still useful in some situations, there are usually better ways to strip panels and bodies if you have access to the necessary skills and equipment.

Category 2

Chemical stripping almost inevitably involves unpleasant, and often dangerous, chemical preparations. In the case of paint removers, it is slow and messy, and often requires one or more re-applications of the chemicals. Paint remover formulations do not attack rust; so separate measures have to be taken to accomplish that task when you use them. They also can result in trapping residues in the crevices of parts and panels that can later leach out and cause lifting of the finishes applied over areas where they were used.

Dip stripping, the high end of chemical paint and rust removal, tends to be an expensive service, and one that is increasingly difficult to find locally. It has the advantage of being very thorough and removing paint and rust in areas that are visible, as well as in areas that cannot be seen. It does this by working its way into the intricacies of complex constructions, such as auto bodies, that cannot be reached by almost any other cleaning method. This may be theoretically desirable, but is rarely absolutely necessary.

The downsides of dip stripping are that it tends to be expensive and its providers are not exactly scattered across the countryside. You may have to stand for the costs and inconvenience of hundreds of miles of two-way transportation for a body that you want cleaned this way.

Although my experience with dip stripping may not be the norm, I

have found that the providers of this service tend to be pretty highhanded when it comes to dealing with individuals who want a body stripped, or even those who want information about their services. Most of these services are mainly in the industrial machinery stripping business, and the providers are often not very good at dealing with the car restoring, fabricating, and customizing public.

Because they have been under attack by various environmental authorities for decades over their disposal of pollutants, dip strippers tend to be secretive and closed-mouthed when you ask them questions. An individual who headed a large dip strip facility once told me bluntly, "We don't discuss proprietary matters." When I pointed out that I was not seeking to know his trade secrets, just some basic consumer information about his service, he terminated the conversation by hanging up on me. My other requests for information about dip stripping from other providers have met less blunt but similarly uncooperative levels of response. It is my firm belief that if a provider does not share information about his or her product or service he/she either doesn't understand it, or has something to hide.

Category 3

In a practical sense, abrasive blasting is limited to air-generated blasting for almost all purposes. I believe that this is the best method to accomplish most automotive part and panel stripping. It is clean and straightforward. Good equipment can be acquired at a relatively low cost, and great equipment is available at somewhat higher costs.

The supplies for abrasive blasting vary greatly in cost, but usable

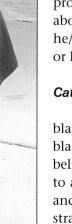

A small blasting setup is ideal for stripping the paint and rust off this hood. In just a few minutes, you are down to sound metal. Note that most of its surface is too complex for any mechanical sanding approach.

This fender is at the edge of what it is practical to disc sand. The damage to it would make it easy to further injure it with a sanding disc. A poly disc would be a better bet. Careful soda and sandblasting are probably the best way to go.

you are stripping. Water and stripped, raw ferrous metals get along all too well. So well that they produce an evil progeny, RUST. To be fair, the water used in wet blasting, and the rinses recommended for after the blasting process is completed, are fortified with rust inhibitors. However, I am not sure that these measures are adequate to prevent rusting under finishes after the fact. Every knowledgeable person in the field of blasting with whom I have discussed this process has had a similar reaction to the concept and practice of wet blasting for auto body stripping. They have been, to say the very least, unenthusiastic.

Blasting Booth Successes

I have seen whole cars stripped with abrasive blasting processes that were performed in varied ways. Here are some examples.

The first blast removal system I ever saw was housed in a blasting booth in a small commercial garage. A 10-hp stationary piston compressor supplied the air. The operator of this facility also painted the vehicles that he stripped. For his sandblasting he used an outside air breathing supply and blasted through a 1/4-inch nozzle. His booth lighting was poor, but his air extraction was excellent. He used bagged sand labeled for masonry use.

It took him a full day to strip a car in his booth. The sand was shoveled after each job, and sorted and separated for reuse. This was many years ago. When plastic media blasting technology arrived, the owner of this facility adopted it, converting the stripping part of his business exclusively to PMB. A couple of years later, he closed his business.

supplies are relatively inexpensive. Acceptable skill levels for basic blasting are fairly easy to master, and people who do a lot of blasting tend to get better at it very quickly.

With the proper approaches, blasting is very thorough at removing almost all contaminants from the accessible surfaces of parts and panels. In the case of in-cabinet blasting, the blasting media can usually be recycled and reused. In the case of outside blasting, the various media that are used tend to be inexpensive and harmless enough to expend without recovery and reuse.

The somewhat new and highly promoted systems for wet blasting with fractured bottle glass have yet to stand the test of time. The claims made by the promoters of this variant of abrasive blasting sound great. However, as far as I know, they remain largely unproven to the full

satisfaction of anyone but those promoters.

Wet blasting may be usable in the long run, or it may not. Certainly, the equipment is too expensive to own on a casual basis. Still, the advertised cost of the wet-blasting service seems low enough; at least it is on a par with the cost of conventional dry abrasive blasting. The potential problem with wet blasting is that very little is generally known about its long-term effects. I have found the willingness of some of its providers to expand the general knowledge of its long-term results in a meaningful and non-promotional way to be meager, at best. Mostly, they tend to deflect any questions regarding these critical issues.

My first reaction to the idea of wet blasting is that water is the last thing you would want to drive into the intricacies of an auto body that

---

Later, I had occasion to visit an outdoor blasting operation on the outskirts of a small village. The air supply was a 3-cylinder diesel compressor that was around 50 to 60 cfm in capacity. The sand was picked up with a dump truck from an undisclosed location and then moved around with a small Bobcat. After several blasting jobs were complete, the sand was spread out in the sun for drying and reuse. Then it was picked up again, sifted, and loaded into a large blast pot for reuse. At this point, the media contained a lot of dust and made quite a cloud when it was used to blast. The individual running this business did not believe in wearing much lung protection. He was not in business for very long.

Another blasting business that I knew a few years back was larger than these two. It used a 750-cfm diesel compressor and had indoor and outdoor blasting capability. The sand was procured directly from a quarry about 40 miles away and used once. After that it was dumped somewhere else. The blast nozzles used here were 3/4-inch.

As you can see, blasting work can be done on many different scales. Some of the smaller equipment to perform it is inexpensive enough to purchase new for occasional work. This equipment has minimal air requirements and is quite slow. Still, if you are blasting one of your own cars every several months or few years, this approach may make sense for you.

Frank's Magic

Does it seem that I am forgetting something in my discussion of abrasive blasting operations that I have known? No, not really. I saved the best for last. Of course, I'm referring to Frank Weinert's approach to blasting, described and illustrated extensively in Chapter 5. Although Frank may not use the shiniest equipment on the planet, or have the most impressive setting, I think that he has the best abrasive blasting process for automobile bodies and parts that I have ever seen.

Perhaps most important is his extensive experience with blasting. He instinctively knows how to adjust his blasting variables to work very efficiently, but without endangering the metal that he is blasting. Frank Weinert's two-step media blasting sequence is the best approach that I have seen. First, his soda blast gets rid of paint and loose rust, revealing areas where more aggressive measures need to be taken. This minimizes the chance of his sandblasting damaging panels when he moves to the sand media phase of his process. Frank's final removal operation uses a small, mechanically driven abrasive pad to remove any remaining deep, pitted rust. This completes the job, again with little chance of distorting or damaging the metal.

In my opinion, the sequence and processes that Frank Weinert uses are the most sensible and effective that I have seen for stripping auto bodies and panels. Although his equipment is ideally suited and sized for the work he does, smaller versions of the same equipment are readily and inexpensively available from several vendors. These might be ideal for your stripping jobs, as well.

Frank Weinert knows metal and blasting. He strips vehicle bodies with three abrasive steps. First, he soda blasts paint and loose rust. Then, he sandblasts any remaining deeper rust. Finally, he mechanically sands any surviving rust spots and pits. His approach is the best that I have seen.